I0016154

Distributed Programming in Ada with Protected Objects

by
Pascal Ledru

ISBN: 1-58112-034-6

DISSERTATION.COM

1998

Copyright © 1998 Pascal Ledru
All rights reserved.

ISBN: 1-58112-034-6

Dissertation.com

1998

www.dissertation.com/library/1120346a.htm

DISTRIBUTED PROGRAMMING IN ADA WITH PROTECTED OBJECTS

by

PASCAL LEDRU

A THESIS

Submitted in partial fulfillment of the requirements
for the degree of Master of Science in
The Department of Computer Science
of
The School of Graduate Studies
of
The University of Alabama in Huntsville

HUNTSVILLE, ALABAMA

1995

ABSTRACT
School of Graduate Studies
The University of Alabama in Huntsville

Degree___Master of Science_____College/Dept. Science / Computer Science

Name of Candidate_Pascal Ledru_____

Title___Distributed Programming in Ada With Protected Objects_____

As distributed applications become more sophisticated, their implementation becomes more and more difficult. It is therefore important to study how to facilitate the implementation of efficient distributed applications. This thesis reviews the different classes of distributed languages and presents a new approach to develop efficient distributed programs using the Ada language. This approach is compared in detail with existing distributed programming languages, existing approaches to distribute Ada programs, and the Distributed Annex of the new revision of the Ada language.

Abstract Approval: Committee Chair   S. G. Shiva   10/26/95

                                        (Date)

                Department Chair   10/30/95

                Graduate Dean   11/6/95

ii

THESIS APPROVAL FORM

Submitted by Pascal Ledru in partial fulfillment of the requirements for the degree of Master of Science with a major in Computer Science.

Accepted on behalf of the Faculty of the School of Graduate Studies by the thesis committee:

S. G. Shiva 10/26/95 Committee Chair
(Date)

Wang Shi 10/26/95

E. A. Reed 10/26/95

_____

_____

_____

_____ Department Chair

_____ College Dean

_____ Graduate Dean

iii

ACKNOWLEDGMENTS

First, I would like to express my gratitude to Dr. Sajjan G. Shiva for his support and guidance as the thesis progressed. He has been very helpful with comments and suggestions. Secondly, I would like to thank the other members of my committee, Dr. Terence J. Reed and Dr. Hui Wang, for their comments.

Last, but not least, I would like to thank my wife Sungmi for all her help and encouragement in the preparation of this thesis, which seemed at times as though it would never end.

TABLE OF CONTENTS

LIST OF FIGURES

LIST OF TABLES

Chapter 1

Introduction

A distributed system is defined as a collection of autonomous computers linked by a network, with software designed to maintain an integrated computing facility. Distributed systems can be programmed using three different methods. The first builds applications directly on top of the hardware. Although this method is highly efficient, it is extremely hardware dependent, difficult to implement, and non-portable. The second uses an existing sequential language plus a collection of operating system primitives. This method is also non-portable since it is operating system dependent. The third uses a programming language containing all the facilities for expressing distributed programs. This method is highly portable and also makes it easy to program by providing a higher level of abstraction.

When distributed systems first appeared, they were programmed using the first and the second methods. As distributed applications became more and more sophisticated, these methods were no longer satisfactory. In order to solve this problem, distributed programming languages have emerged. Distributed languages can be divided into two categories: languages with *logically distributed address space* and languages with *logically shared address space*. The latter has the advantage of hiding complexity of communication over the former.

Ada is a language which supports communication of sequential processes [Hoare, 1978], and therefore should be able to support distributed systems programming. Ada has a tasking mechanism, and according to the Ada Reference Manual [Ada 95 Reference Manual], it is possible for tasks to be distributed within an Ada program. Parallel tasks may be implemented on *multicomputers*, on multiprocessors, or with interleaved execution on a single physical processor. Extensive studies have been undertaken to distribute Ada programs, and several authors pointed out that the Ada 83 Reference Manual was incomplete regarding the distributed issues [Volz et al., 1987] [Volz et al., 1989]. Due to the incompleteness of Ada 83, Ada 95 contains an annex based on the *Remote Procedure Call* paradigm. It describes a model for execution of programs on distributed systems.

Another enhancement of Ada 95 is a new feature, the *protected object,* which is intended for synchronized access to data on shared memory systems. Even though the protected object is intended for a shared memory system, the future of the computer technology lies in the distributed environment. With this in mind, this thesis examines the possible implementation of *distributed protected objects*. There are existing languages which support concept similar to the protected object over a logically shared address space. But these languages (e.g., Occam and Linda) suffer from the following limitations: they are experimental and often architecture dependent compared to Ada. Therefore, for this thesis, Ada was the choice for implementing distributed protected objects.

The thesis is organized as follows. Chapter two reviews characteristics of several distributed programming languages and shows the advantages of the *logically shared address space* paradigm over the *logically distributed address space* paradigm. Chapter three first reviews how Ada 83 implements distributed programs and points out limitations of the language. Secondly, Annex E, Distributed Systems of Ada 95, is closely reviewed. The chapter ends with the introduction of a new model: distributed protected objects. Chapter four presents the implementation of the model. Chapter 5 concludes the thesis.

Chapter 2

Distributed Programming Languages

As stated previously, distributed applications can be built directly on top of the hardware, on top of an operating system, or in a special language for distributed programming. The first method provides total control over all primitives provided by the hardware, such as interfaces to communication devices. Although this method allows efficient utilization of the available resources, it has the severe disadvantage of being hardware dependent, and hence is not practical for developing large software systems.

The second method uses an existing sequential language plus a collection of operating system primitives accessed through library routines. Applications developed using this method can be made hardware independent, but they will always be operating system dependent.

The third method employs a programming language containing all the necessary constructs for expressing distributed programs. This method shields the application programmer from both the operating system and the hardware. As a second major advantage, such a programming language can ease the programming task by presenting a higher level, more abstract model of a distributed system.

Many languages for distributed programming have already been developed and implemented. A closer look at these languages is the main subject of this chapter. But before examining some of these languages which represent different classes in detail, this chapter reviews how parallelism and communication and synchronization are supported in distributed systems, programmed with or without language support.

2.1 Importance of Language Support for Programming Distributed Systems

A distributed application can be characterized by parallelism, and interprocess communication and synchronization. Distributed applications differ from their sequential counterparts in such a way that the former contain sections of code which run in parallel. Among different sections of the code exchange of information may be necessary, and thus requires communication and synchronization between the sections. Due to the fact that parallel portions are independent of each other, failure of one should not prevent the rest from continuing their execution. The following sections examine parallelism, and interprocess communication and synchronization in detail and show why it is important to provide language support.

2.1.1 Parallelism

In most distributed operating systems, the unit of parallelism is a process. The Unix *fork* system call creates a process with an execution environment copied from the parent process which executed the system call. The *exec* call transforms the calling process into the one executing the code of a named program. The *rexec* and *rsh* calls extend the exec call to remote calls. All these system calls can provide a user with parallelism, but it is the user's responsibility to distribute work among different processes using these system calls. On the other hand, there are languages which have parallelism built in. For example, in Occam [Inmos, 1984], there is a construct called *statements*. These statements can be executed either sequentially, as in

```
SEQ
    S1
    S2
```

or in parallel, as in

```
PAR
    S1
    S2
```

In a pure functional language, functions behave like mathematical functions: they compute a result that depends only on their input data. Such functions do not have *side effects*. If functions do not have any side effect, the order in which they are executed makes no difference. For example, in the expression

h(f(3,4), g(8))

it is possible to evaluate f and g in parallel [Hudak, 1986].

Logic programs can be read *declaratively* as well as *procedurally*. In the code below, two *clauses* for the predicate A are given:

(1) A :- B,C,D.

(2) A :- E,F.

The declarative reading of the clauses is "if B,C and D are true, then A is true"(Clause (1)) and "if E and F are true, then A is true"(Clause (2)). Procedurally, the clauses can be interpreted as "to prove theorem A, you either have to prove subtheorems B, C, and D, or you have to prove subtheorems E and F." From the procedural readings, it becomes clear that there are two opportunities for parallelism:

(1) *OR-parallelism* - The two clauses for A can be worked on in parallel until one of them succeeds or both fail.

(2) *AND-parallelism* - For each of the two clauses, the subtheorems can be worked on in parallel until they all succeed or any one of them fails.

As seen in the previous examples, built-in parallelism of a distributed language can determine which parts can be executed in parallel. And there are also languages which support concepts similar to processes provided by an operating system, as a part of language definition. For example, Ada supports *tasks*. The main advantage of having such constructs is portability.

2.1.2 Interprocess Communication and Synchronization

In most distributed operating systems, distributed processes communicate by *message passing*, and operating systems typically support two forms of message passing mechanisms: Blocking or non-blocking primitives, and reliable or non-reliable primitives. Even though some operating systems provide higher level of abstractions such as *Remote Procedure Call* (RPC) or broadcasting, these are operating system specific. In hybrid environment, it is not easy to distribute work across different operating systems. For instance, an operating system supporting RPC (Amoeba) cannot communicate with another supporting only message passing primitives (Unix) unless much work is done to simulate RPC. Programs written on top of a specific system are therefore difficult to port to other systems. [Bal, 1990a] gives a specific example of the difficulties encountered in porting an application developed for the Crystal multicomputer which uses asynchronous message passing to Amoeba which uses (synchronous) RPC. Another area in which distributed operating systems are not adequate is *strong type checking*. Distributed operating systems only support exchange of byte streams; they do not check whether the sender and the receiver are interpreting the parameters consistently. In addition, problems arise while trying to send a complex data structure such as a tree. Usually, the programmer has to write a subprogram to convert the data structure to a sequence of bytes.

The problems described above can be minimized if interprocess communication is directly supported by languages. Languages provide interprocess communication by *message passing* and *shared data*. The message passing allows two entities to communicate with each other by exchanging the data explicitly. The shared data can be conceived as a mailbox. A process deposits data and the other retrieves, and thus interprocess communication occurs implicitly.

In message passing, there are two issues of importance. The first issue is how the sender and the receiver address each other. In the simplest case, both the sender and the receiver explicitly name each other. Requiring the receiver to specify the sender of the message is rather inflexible, precluding the possibility of receiving messages from any other client (for example, a file server). A solution is to allow the receiver to accept messages sent by any process. This form is called asymmetric direct naming. Another solution is indirect naming which uses an intermediate object, like a port rather than process names. Ports are more flexible than direct naming since neither the sender nor the receiver needs to know the identity of the other. The second issue concerns synchronous versus asynchronous message passing. Both use *send* and *receive* primitives but differ depending on when the sender continues. With synchronous message passing, the sender waits until the message has been delivered at the receiving process; i.e., the receiver has finished executing the *receive* statement and has stored the message in its local variable. With asynchronous message passing, the sender continues immediately after issuing the *send* statement. Synchronous message passing is simpler to use, because when the sender continues it knows the message has been processed. But synchronous message passing is more restrictive since the sender blocks until the receiver receives the message. Some languages support both synchronous and asynchronous communication (e.g., SR). Other languages (e.g., CSP, Occam, Ada 83) provide only synchronous message passing.

The send and the receive operations used above transfer information in one direction, from the sender to the receiver. In many cases, the receiver wants to return a reply to the sender. With the send and the receive primitives, the programmer needs two messages, one for each direction. An alternative is to use a single message passing construct that transfers data in both directions. Two-way interactions occur in the *client-server* model.

The client sends a request and the server returns a reply. Two widely used message passing mechanisms based on this principle are the *rendezvous* and the *remote procedure call.*

The rendezvous mechanism is based on two-way message passing and explicit message receipt. With the rendezvous, the receiver (server) contains operations that senders (clients) can request to execute. Such procedures are called *entries* in Ada. The declaration of an entry is similar to that of a procedure. If a client issues a request to execute an entry, it is said to do an entry call. The client now blocks until the entry call has been processed by the server and it has received the result of the call.

Like the rendezvous, the Remote Procedure Call is based on two-way message passing. The idea behind RPC is to allow communication between the client and the server through conventional procedure calls, even if they are on different machines. The Remote Procedure Call mechanism is described in detail by [Birrel and Nelson, 1984].

Parallel programming languages on *tightly coupled* (shared memory) systems use not only mechanisms such as the rendezvous or other forms of message passing, but also shared variables. Variables are defined as *shared* if they can be accessed or modified by several threads. In order to ensure integrity of the shared variables, the access must be explicitly synchronized. The synchronization on these shared variables is usually ensured by low-level primitives such as *semaphores, monitors,* or *critical sections* which are easy to misuse and can lead to programs which are difficult to maintain. Shared data is defined as an abstract data type which encapsulates both variables and operations on these variables. Operations defined on these shared data enforce synchronization implicitly, and thus is hidden from the users.

The shared data concept also can be extended to parallel programming languages on *loosely coupled* (distributed memory) systems. At first glance, it may seem unnatural to use shared data for communication among distributed systems, as such systems do not have physically shared memory. Nevertheless, the shared data paradigm provides several advantages over message passing. A message passing mechanism is usually used to communicate between two processes. On the other hand, shared data can be used to communicate among any number of processes. A process which updates shared data does not need to know the location of the other processes using the shared data [Bal and Tanenbaum, 1988]. Finally, an assignment to a shared data has immediate effect; i.e., it guarantees *order-preserving*; such order-preserving may be harder to obtain if several processes communicate using a message passing mechanism [Bal and Tanenbaum, 1988].

The shared data model can also be viewed as an abstraction layer over the *distributed shared memory* (DSM). The DSM provides a virtual address space shared among processes on loosely coupled processors [Nitzberg and Lo, 1991]. In DSM, replication is usually used in order to improve performance, and the unit of replication is a physical page. Of course, like the shared variables described above, since multiple processors can access the DSM, data synchronization has to be explicitly provided. Conversely, the shared data model is integrated in a programming language, and it is superior to the DSM model in terms of programmability and readability. Better performance can be achieved [Levelt et al., 1992] since only the shared data are replicated instead of physical pages [Bal et al., 1992b].

Several languages support the shared data model using different mechanisms. These languages are *Shared Logical Variables* in Parlog, *Tuple Space* in Linda, *Shared Data Objects* in Orca, *Protected Objects* in Ada 95, *Capsules* in Concurrent C/C++, *Classes* in Distributed Eiffel, and *Resources* in Pascal-FC [Burns and Davies, 1992]. In the following sections, Linda, Orca, Ada 95, Concurrent C/C++, and Distributed Eiffel are discussed in detail; Ada 95 is also discussed in detail in the following chapters. Some implementation details of the Shared data objects model of Orca are also presented.

2.2 Languages for Programming Distributed Systems

The languages reviewed in this thesis are categorized into three: languages using a message passing mechanism, languages using a shared data mechanism, and languages using both mechanisms. Each category of languages is further partitioned into a number of classes. The classification is illustrated in Figure 2.1.

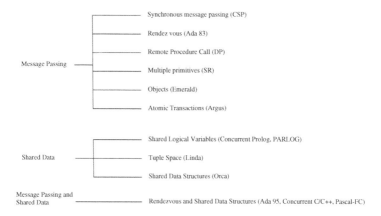

Figure 2.1. Classification of languages for distributed programming

For each language, the following sections describe how parallelism, communication, and synchronization are expressed in the language, and how parallel units are mapped onto processors if the language addresses this issue. For some languages, some implementation details are also given.

2.2.1 Languages using a message passing mechanism

This section presents several languages supporting message passing, rendezvous, RPC and multiple communication primitives.

2.2.1.1 Message Passing - CSP

The Communicating Sequential Processes (CSP) [Hoare, 1978] model consists of a fixed number of sequential processes that communicate only through synchronous message passing.

Parallelism: CSP provides a simple parallel command to create a fixed number of parallel processes. CSP processes take no parameters and cannot be mapped onto specific processors. An array of similar processes can be created, but their number must be a compile time constant.

Communication and Synchronization: CSP processes may not communicate through global variables. All interprocess communication is done using synchronous receive and send. The sending process specifies the name of the destination process and provides a value to be sent. The receiving process specifies the name of the sending process and provides a variable to which the received value is assigned. A process executing either a send or a receive is blocked until its partner has executed the complementary statement.

2.2.1.2 Rendezvous - Ada 83

Ada 83 supports applications that can use multiple processes and run on *multicomputers*, on multiprocessors, or with interleaved execution on a single physical processor [Ada Programming Language].

Parallelism: Ada provides the task as the unit of parallelism. Tasks are identical to a process, and they can be created dynamically.

Communication and Synchronization: Ada tasks communicate by using the rendezvous mechanism and by global variables. Tasks synchronize with each other during a rendezvous; then they continue their normal execution independently of each other. A task can call an entry of another task by using an *entry call statement*, similar to a procedure call. An entry call specifies the name of the task containing the entry as well as the entry name itself. Ada uses a *select statement* for expressing nondeterminism. Ada's select statement is used for three different purposes: to select an entry call nondeterministically from a set of requests, to call an entry conditionally (i.e., only if the called task is ready to accept it immediately), and to set a timeout on an entry call.

2.2.1.3 Remote Procedure Call - Distributed Processes [Brinch Hansen, 1978]

Parallelism: In Distributed Processes (DP), the number of processes is fixed at compile time. The intention is to dedicate one processor to execute each process. Each process, however, can contain several threads of control. A process definition contains an initial statement which may be empty if this is the first thread; a thread may continue forever, or it may finish executing at some point. But in either case the process itself continues to exist; DP processes never terminate. Additional threads are initiated by calls from other processes. Arrays of processes may be declared. A process can determine its array index using the built-in function*this*.

Communication and Synchronization: DP processes communicate by calling the other's common procedures. Such a call has the form: call P.f(exprs, vars) where P is the name of the called process and f is the name of a procedure declared by P. The expressions such as exprs are input parameters; the return values such as vars of the call are assigned to the output variables. The calling process and all its threads are blocked during the call. A new thread of control is created within the called process P.

2.2.1.4 Multiple communication primitives - SR

Synchronization Resources (SR) [Andrews et al., 1988] is based on Modula, Pascal, and DP, and provides several models of interprocess communication.

Parallelism: An SR program consists of one or more *resources*. A resource is a module which runs on one physical node (either a single processor or a shared memory multiprocessor). Resources are dynamically created and optionally assigned to run on a specific machine. An identifier for the resource instance is returned by the *create* command. A resource can contain several processes, and these may share data. Synchronization among these processes is supported by the use of semaphores. Communication with processes in other resources is restricted to *operations*. A resource may contain an initialization and a termination process. These are created and run implicitly. A resource terminates when it is killed by the *destroy* command. A program terminates when all its processes terminate or block.

Communication and Synchronization: An SR operation definition looks like a procedure definition. Its implementation can either look like a procedure or an entry point. When implemented as a procedure, the operation is serviced by an implicitly created process. When implemented as an entry point, it is serviced by an already running process in a rendezvous. The two types of implementation are transparent to the invoker of the operation. On the invoker's side, an operation may be called asynchronously using a *send* or synchronously using a *call*. Several calls can be grouped in a parallel call-statement, which terminates when all calls have been completed. The operation and its resource instance must be named explicitly in the invocation. This is done using the identifier for the resource returned by the *create* command. By combining the two modes of servicing operations and the two modes of invoking them, four types of interprocess communications can be expressed.

SR uses a construct similar to the Ada *select* statement to deal with nondeterminism. The SR's *guarded command*, or *alternative,* has the following form:

```
entry_point(params) and bool-expr by expr -> statements
```

Within an operation, a guarded command may contain an entry point, a Boolean expression, and a priority expression. An alternative is enabled if there is a pending invocation of the guarded command and the Boolean expression associated with it evaluates to true. The expression in the *by* part (`by expr -> statements`) is used for priorization when there are several pending invocations of the same guarded command. If all Boolean expressions are false, the process suspends.

2.2.1.5 Object oriented languages - Emerald

Emerald [Black et al., 1987] is an object-based programming language for the implementation of distributed applications. Emerald considers all entities to be objects. For the programmer, both a file accessible by many processes and a Boolean variable local to a single process are objects. Objects are either passive or active. Emerald is categorized as *object based* since it does not support inheritance. Abstract types are used to define the interface to an object.

Parallelism: Parallelism is based on simultaneous execution of active objects. The language supports process migration by moving objects from one processor to another. Such a move may be initiated either by the compiler using compile time analysis or by the programmer using language primitives.

Communication and Synchronization: An object consists of four parts: a name, a representation, a set of operations, and an optional process. The name uniquely identifies the object within the distributed system. The representation contains the data of the object. Objects communicate by invoking each other's operations. There can be multiple active invocations within one object. The optional process runs in parallel to all these invocations. The invocations and the data shared among them can be encapsulated in a monitor construct. The internal process can enter the monitor by calling an operation of its own object. Emerald provides the same semantics for local and remote invocations.

2.2.2 Languages using a shared data mechanism

As opposed to the message passing mechanism, data sharing has several advantages in interprocess communication. This section reviews some languages based on a shared data mechanism.

2.2.2.1 Distributed Data Structures - Linda

Linda [Ahuja et al., 1986] [Carriero and Gerlernter, 1989] consists of a set of primitives which can be integrated into another language, such as C or Ada, and provides parallelism to the existing language. Linda limits itself to four constructions and the notion of *Tuple Space*. The Tuple Space is the core component of Linda, and this data structure may be distributed. Distributed activities can use Linda for communication and synchronization. The Tuple Space stores a collection of tuples, and processes produce and consume tuples. A tuple is an ordered set of heterogeneous elements which are called *fields*. A consumer waits until a producer drops a matching tuple in the Tuple Space, and this is the way it expresses synchronization and communication.

(1) Parallelism. Linda provides a simple primitive called *eval* to create a sequential process. Linda does not have a notation for mapping processes to processors.

(2) Communication and Synchronization. *Out* drops a tuple in the Tuple Space. *Rd* reads a tuple without removing it from the Tuple Space. *In* reads a tuple and removes it from the Tuple Space. For example:

```
out("tuple1",1,false)
in("tuple1", int i, bool b)
rd("tuple1", int i, bool b)
```

All these operations are atomic; i.e., they are not interrupted until completion.

2.2.3 Languages using Distributed Shared Data Objects

As shown in the previous section, Linda provides only a fixed number of operations: add, read, and delete. Users cannot define their own operations. Also, Linda's support for complex data structures like sets and graphs is low level. [Bal et al., 1992a] draws attention to the complexity of building complex operations with Linda: "The operations allowed on Tuple Space are low-level and built-in, which complicates programming and makes an efficient distributed implementation difficult." As an alternative, [Bal et al., 1992a] introduces the shared data object model and the language Orca which is designed for highly parallel programs. The following section discusses it in detail. There are also languages such as Distributed Eiffel, Ada 95, and Concurrent C/C++ using similar models which are also presented in this section.

2.2.3.1 Orca

Orca was designed for highly parallel programs. Its designers concluded that for their purposes, it was desirable to have explicit programmer-controlled parallelism and implicit communication through logically shared data, and that partial failures should be dealt with by the implementation provided that the cost for doing so is justifiable [Bal, 1990a]. Replication is the key to efficient sharing of data in Orca; nevertheless, having multiple copies of the same data may introduce inconsistency problems if several processes simultaneously try to access the same shared data structure. In Orca, *mutual exclusion* is done implicitly by executing all operations on objects *indivisibly*. The model guarantees *serializability* of operation invocations: when two operations are applied simultaneously to the same data-object, even though the order is nondeterministic, the result is same as that of sequential execution of the operations. Orca also provides conditional synchronization which allows a process to wait until a certain condition becomes true.

Parallelism: The unit of parallelism in Orca is the process. A process definition in Orca consists of a name, parameter specification, and body:

```
process name(formal-parameters);
  local declaractions
begin
  statements
end;
```

New processes are created explicitly through the fork statement:

```
fork name(actual-parameters);
fork name(actual-parameters) on (processor-number);
```

Communication and Synchronization: Processes in Orca communicate through shared data objects. The type of such an object is essentially an *abstract data type*, as it defines a number of operations on data but hides the actual implementation of the data structure and the operations. The syntax of the shared data object is composed of a *specification* part and an *implementation* part, and is as follows:

```
object specification name;
  operation op1(formal-parameters) : ResultType;
  operation op2(formal-parameters) : ResultType;
  ...
end;
object implementation name;
  declaration for internal data
  operation op1(formal-parameters) : ResultType;
    local declarations of op1
  begin
    code for op1
  end;
  operation op2(formal-parameters) : ResultType;
    local declarations of op2
  begin
    code for op2
  end;
  ...
begin
  code that initializes internal data
end;
```

As stated before, operations may block until a certain condition becomes true, and it can be expressed as follows. The operation invocation blocks until one or more of the conditions are true. Next, one true condition is selected nondeterministically and its corresponding statements are executed.

```
operation op(formal-parameters) : ResultType;
  local declarations
begin
  guard condition_1 do statements_1 od;
  guard condition_2 do statements_2 od;
  ...
  guard condition_n do statements_n od;
end;
```

The following is an actual example of a shared data object. The name of the object in this example is IntObject, and it defines three operations: Value, Assign, and AwaitValue. The operation Value() returns the current value of the object. The operation Assign() assigns new value to the object. And the operation AwaitValue() waits until the value of the object is equal to the value passed in by parameter.

```
object specification IntObject;
  operation Value(): integer;          # return value
  operation Assign(v : integer);       # assign new value
  operation AwaitValue(v : integer);   # wait for certain value
end;
object implementation IntObject;
  x : integer; # internal data
  operation Value(): integer;
  begin
    return x;
  end;
  operation Assign(v: integer);
  begin
    x := v;
  end;
  operation AwaitValue(v : integer);
  begin
    guard x = v do od;
  end;
begin
  x := 0;
end;
```

Data structures: Orca was specifically designed for distributed systems, and hence it only supports data structures that are secure and suitable for distribution. For example, the designers of Orca excluded the use of pointers which, if implemented as addresses, are only meaningful within a single machine.

Implementation: A simple implementation of the shared data-object will locate each object at a given location; processes will access the shared data-objects using Remote Procedure Calls. This implementation will incur a huge communication overhead since the access to the shared data object is centralized and can create bottlenecks. A better implementation of Orca [Bal et al., 1992a] avoids the problem by replicating objects. It is useful to distinguish between *read* operations and *write* operations on replicated data. In Orca, a read operation is an operation that does not change the internal data of the object it is applied to; a write operation changes the internal data of the object it is applied to. The primary goal of replicating shared data-objects is to apply read operations to a local copy of the object, without doing any interprocess communication. On a write operation, all copies of the object must be updated, so a write operation involves communication. The second goal of replication is to increase parallelism. If an object is stored on only one processor, every operation has to be executed by that processor which causes a bottleneck.

The other implementation [Bal and Kaashoek, 1993] is a combination of the two previous implementations. In the second implementation above, it is costly to replicate the shared data if the majority of the operations on the object are write operations. So, if read-write ratio is low, an object is stored in one processor and the other processors access it through RPC. But the communication overhead can be reduced by allowing migration of the object to nearby processes which are likely to access the object the most. If read-write ratio is high, an object is replicated in multiple machines. Replication or migration are based on compile-time information, run-time information, or a combination of both.

A major problem which occurs in a distributed system using replication techniques is to ensure that all processes observe changes to shared objects *in the same order*. [Kaashoek et al., 1989] describes the *update protocol* based on *reliable broadcast* used by Orca. To emphasize the necessity of a reliable broadcast, consider the following example: among a number of processes, two of them, each on a different machine, simultaneously broadcast two messages, A and B respectively. If a reliable broadcast protocol is not used, some processes will receive A first and others B first. At the end, the former has message B while the latter has message A, causing data inconsistency; all the processes should either have A or B. The basic reliable broadcast protocol used by Orca works as follows. When an application process wants to broadcast a message M, it first sends this message to a *sequencer* using an ordinary point-to-point communication protocol. When the sequencer receives the point-to-point message M, it allocates a sequence number n and broadcasts a packet containing M and n. All broadcasts are issued from the same node, by the sequencer which ensures serializability. The sequencer stores old broadcast messages in its *history buffer*. When the history buffer becomes full, the sequencer enters a resynchronization phase. If a node misses a message, when the following message eventually arrives, the node notices a gap in the sequence numbers. It was expecting n next, and it received $n+1$, so it knows it has missed one. The node then sends a special point-to-point message to the sequencer asking for the missing message stored in the history buffer.

Examples: Several examples are described in [Bal, 1991], and [Bal and Kaashoek, 1993]. These examples include matrix multiplication, the *All-Pair Shortest Paths* (ASP) problem, and the *Successive overrelaxation* (SOR) problem.

The matrix multiplication algorithm is straightforward. Basically, each processor computes one or more rows of the result matrix.

In the ASP problem, it is desired to find the length of the shortest path from any node i to another node j in a given graph. The standard sequential algorithm uses a sequence of matrices for storing the lengths of all the paths. After iteration k, element $C^k(i, j)$ contains the length of the shortest path from i to j found so far (i.e., the best path visiting only nodes 1 to k). This sequential algorithm can be transformed into a parallel algorithm by computing the rows of the matrix $C^k(i, j)$ in parallel.

SOR is an iterative method for solving discretized Laplace equations on a grid. The sequential SOR algorithm works as follows. During each iteration, the algorithm considers all non-boundary points of the grid. For each point, SOR first computes the average value of its four neighbors. Next, it determines the new value of the point. A parallel algorithm treats the grid as a checkerboard and alernately updates all black points and all red points. As each point has only neighbors of the opposite color, each update phase can easily be parallelized.

In these examples, Orca achieves an almost perfect speedup on a distributed system containing 10 nodes that are connected by a 10 Mbit/sec Ethernet.

2.2.3.2 Distributed Eiffel

Distributed Eiffel [Gunasselan and LeBlanc, 1992] is a language that allows distributed applications to run on the *Clouds* [Dasgupta et al., 1991] operating system. Distributed Eiffel takes advantage of the DSM capabilities of Clouds.

(1) Parallelism. In Distributed Eiffel, parallelism is based on the notion of *threads*. An application can have more than one thread, some of which may be active within the same object, while some are active in different objects.

(2) Communication and Synchronization. Threads communicate with each other by *object*. To address the issue of synchronization among multiple threads that potentially

access or update the state information within an object, the language provides multiple readers-a single writer model of synchronization which can be combined with conditional synchronization. A conditional synchronization scheme allows a thread to wait for some condition to become true. Objects in Distributed Eiffel are similar to the Shared Data Objects of Orca.

2.2.3.3 Ada 95

Ada 95 offers two forms of communication: the rendezvous model and the *protected objects* model. A study of the rendezvous mechanism was presented in the description of Ada 83. In this section, the discussion is focused on protected objects. Protected objects are very similar to the Shared Data Objects of Orca but were intended for shared memory systems. A protected object is a lightweight, data oriented synchronization mechanism; it encapsulates shared data and protected operations. A protected object has private components. These components are intended to be shared among concurrent tasks. Like tasks, protected objects may be either protected types or single protected objects. Like task types, protected objects are limited types; they both support discriminants and entries families.

Three forms of operations are possible on a protected object: *protected functions, protected procedures*, and *entries*. Functions are for read-only accesses, and therefore, if a task is executing a function, any other task accessing the same protected object can only execute functions. Procedures and entries are for read/write accesses, and therefore, if a task is executing a procedure or an entry, any other task is excluded from the protected object. The difference between procedures and entries is that the latter has a *barrier condition* which must be true before the entry body can be executed; otherwise, the entry is queued. The number of tasks waiting on an entry queue is implicitly maintained by the

Count attribute of the entry. Barrier conditions are reevaluated after completion of a protected procedure or an entry body since a task which had been queued on a false barrier may be able to proceed due to the change of the state of the object. Therefore, already queued entries take precedence over external calls contending for the protected object. In other terms, the barrier protection mechanism superimposes itself upon the mutual exclusion mechanism of the protected object, thus giving two distinct level of protection and solving race condition problems [Barnes, 1994].

The following example illustrates the use of protected objects. A protected object Counter provides three operations: a function (Value_Of) to return the current value of the object, a procedure (Increment) to increment its value, and an entry (Decrement) to decrement its value. The protected object is decomposed into a specification and an implementation. The specification lists the operations that can be applied to the object and specifies the protected data (Data) of the object. The implementation details the implementation of the operations.

```
protected Counter is
  procedure Increment( New_Value : out NATURAL);
  entry Decrement( New_Value : out NATURAL);
  function Value_Of return NATURAL;
private
  Data : NATURAL := 0;
end Counter;
protected body Counter is
  procedure Increment( New_Value : out NATURAL) is
  begin -- Increment
    Data := Data + 1;
  end Increment;
  entry Decrement( New_Value : out NATURAL) when Data > 0 is
  begin -- Decrement
    Data := Data -1;
  end Decrement;
  function Value_Of is
  begin -- Value_Of
    return Data;
  end Value_Of;
end Counter;
```

Another important feature of protected objects is the *requeue* statement. The effect of the requeue statement is to refer the caller of an entry to another entry. This is not a procedure call since control does not return to the statement following the requeue. The requeue statement provides the ability to offer a service in two parts, where a calling task is suspended after the first part until conditions are such that the second part can proceed [Barnes, 1994]. An example of a usage of the requeue statement is to implement protected objects with entry barriers depending on parameters of the entries [Ledru, 1995b].

Protected Objects are expected to provide an extremely efficient mechanism, and several rules ensure that they can be implemented efficiently. Important things to note [Ada 95 Rationale] are:

- Protected subprograms do not have barriers. Protected entries always have barriers.

- Barriers are associated with entry queues, not with individual tasks calling the entries; therefore an entry barrier can not depend on the parameters of the entries.

- Entry barriers are reevaluated only when an entry is queued and when an entry or a protected procedure has just finished.

- Barriers and protected operation bodies should contain only short, bounded-time expressions, and they are not allowed to call potentially blocking operations.

- Calls on protected objects' entries as calls on tasks' entries can be cancelled if they are not selected immediately (conditional entry calls), or if they are not selected before an expiration time is reached (timed entry calls).

Protected objects are built on the concepts of two other synchronization primitives: conditional critical regions and monitors, and they can be viewed as an amalgam of the best features of these two primitives. The characteristics of protected objects are described in greater detail in [Ada 95 Rationale] and [Barnes, 1994].

Ada 95 also contains a Distributed Systems annex describing a model for execution of the programs on distributed systems. This annex is reviewed in detail in the following chapter.

2.2.3.4 Concurrent C/C++

Concurrent C/C++ extends the C++ language by adding support for distributing programming.

Parallelism: A process in Concurrent C/C++ [Gehani, 1993] has a specification and a body, like tasks in Ada. The specification part consists of the process's name, a list of parameters, and a list of entries. Processes are created explicitly, using the *create* primitive.

Communication and Synchronization: Processes communicate through the rendezvous and the *capsule* mechanisms. Capsules are very similar to the Shared Data Objects of Orca but support inheritance and have more flexible guard expressions.

2.3 Summary

The first section reviewed how to program distributed systems without language support. This approach is operating system dependent and therefore not portable.

The second section reviewed how parallelism, and interprocess communication and synchronization are provided by distributed languages. This section showed that data sharing can be used on loosely coupled systems and that it provides a higher level of abstraction than message passing. The main advantage of data sharing is that it can be used to communicate among any number of processes.

The last section reviewed several languages for distributed programming. Each of these languages is representative of a class of distributed languages. Languages based on message passing are relatively low level models, and they do not hide details of communication. Languages based on shared data allow processes to share information easily and provide a higher level of abstraction than languages based on message passing. Shared logical variables are used by logic programming languages. If these languages provide a high level of abstraction, their implementations are still relatively inefficient. The Tuple Space model has simple and clean semantics, but it does not support complex data structures. The Shared Data Object model has been especially designed for programming distributed systems, and implementation of this model is very efficient. Languages based on both mechanisms provide the advantages of the shared data mechanism but still provide message passing which may be needed while programming one-to-one communication applications. Languages such as CSP and DP only support message passing while more recent languages such as Linda and Orca only support shared data. Emerging languages such as Concurrent C/C++ and Ada 95 support both mechanisms. Ada 95 supports rendezvous which are used for synchronous communication between a pair of tasks and protected objects which provide synchronized access to shared data. The Protected Object model is very similar to the Shared Data Object model. Implementing protected objects in a distributed environment will provide the advantages of both Orca and Ada. Such an implementation is the subject of the next chapters.

Chapter 3

Ada as a Language For Programming Distributed Systems

The previous chapter compared two interprocess communication mechanisms: message passing and data sharing, and evaluated several languages using these primitives. It concluded that data sharing provided a higher level of abstraction than message passing. This chapter presents how to use Ada to program distributed systems and introduces a new model of distribution based on data sharing.

Ada 83 recognizes the possibility of executing a single Ada program on *multicomputers*. Several approaches and methodologies [Bishop et al., 1987] [Bishop, 1988] have been proposed to distribute a single program over a network of computers, and considerable work has been done to evaluate which units (e.g., tasks or packages) are adequate for distribution [Wellings, 1988] [Volz et al., 1989].

A number of distributed systems have been developed. These systems can be categorized into two classes: *pre-partitioning* systems and *post-partitioning* systems. Pre-partitioning systems require the developer to specify how units must be distributed while writing a program. These systems are based on the concept of *virtual nodes* [Tedd, 1984] [Volz, 1990]. A virtual node is an abstraction of a physical node, and it is defined as one or more units sharing memory and communicating with other virtual nodes only by well defined interfaces. Direct access to data of other nodes is prohibited. Some of these systems [Fisher and Weatherly, 1986] [Atkinson et al., 1988] [Atkinson and Goldsack, 1988] use the remote rendezvous paradigm to communicate among virtual nodes, while others [Volz et al., 1995] use the remote procedure call paradigm. There are other systems [Hutcheon and Wellings, 1989] which use both paradigms. Post-partitioning systems do not force the developer to specify how units must be distributed while writing a program but make use of an *Ada Program Partitioning Language* to specify the partitioning of a program after its design. A system using this approach is described by [Eisenhauer et al., 1989a] [Eisenhauer et al., 1989b] and [Jha et al., 1989]. Both pre-partitioning and post-partitioning systems have shown that several problems occur while distributing a single program, due to the syntax of the language itself. Some of these problems are: timed entry calls [Volz et al., 1985] [Volz and Mudge, 1987], passing access variables as arguments in remote calls [Volz et al., 1989], and references to shared variables [Volz et al., 1989]. Extensions to the language have been proposed to overcome these problems. [Jessop, 1982] introduces the notion of package types. [Atkinson et al., 1990] and [Atkinson, 1991] extend Ada 83 to provide object-oriented features to enhance distribution. [Goldsack et al., 1993] [Goldsack et al., 1994] and [Gargaro et al., 1994] introduce new language constructs to support the development of secure distributed systems. [Dobbing, 1993] proposes a new model of distribution.

Using some of the concepts developed by the systems mentioned above, the new revision of the language called Ada 95 introduces the idea of a *partition* (a form of virtual node) whereby one coherent "program" is distributed over a network of computers. Ada 95 does not include any specific constructs to support distributed programming, but the

Distributed Systems Annex of the language introduces a set of pragmas and packages to distribute Ada programs.

In the following sections the Distributed Systems Annex of the language is reviewed, and some of the restrictions of the Annex are pointed out. A new model based on protected objects and overcoming some of these restrictions is then presented.

3.1 The Ada 95 model

Distributed programming in Ada 95 [Annotated Ada 95 Reference Manual] [Volz et al., 1994] is based on the concept of partitions which communicate with each other through remote procedure call and shared memory. A distributed Ada 95 program is composed of one or more partitions. There are two types of partition: active and passive. Active partitions are aggregations of units that may have state and active threads of control. Passive partitions are aggregations of units with data and any necessary operations on these data. Passive partitions are used to provide a mechanism for sharing data among active partitions, and they have no independent thread of control. Passive partitions provide data (and possibly code) visible to one or more active partitions. A distributed program is configured by assigning the partitions to physical nodes in the system. At a lower level, individual program units (e.g., packages and subprograms) are assigned to the partitions and exist on a node only if they are included in a partition configured on that node. Two types of nodes exist: processing nodes and storages nodes. An active partition must be placed on a processing node while a passive partition can be placed on a processing node or a storage node.

The call interface into an active partition is specified by *remote call interface* (RCI) packages while the interface to a passive partition is specified by a *shared passive* package. Communication to RCI packages is supported by a *Partition Communication Subsystem* (PCS).

An RCI package is a package in which a pragma *Remote_Call_Interface* is included. Associated with the pragma are several constraints that the package must satisfy. For example, an RCI package specification must be preelaborable (there must be little or no run-time elaboration code) and must not contain the declaration of variables. Two related packages are assumed to be generated for each RCI package specification, a *calling stub* and a *receiving stub*. The calling stub replaces the RCI package in all partitions that make remote calls to that RCI package. The calling stub uses the PCS to perform a remote procedure call (RPC) to the receiving stub, which becomes part of the partition containing the RCI package being called. The purpose of the receiving stub is to make the actual call to the called subprogram.

As mentioned above, the interface to passive partitions is specified by *shared passive* packages. Restrictions on shared passive packages are intended to eliminate the need for a separate run-time system on these partitions. For example, shared passive packages may not contain tasks and protected objects with entries. [Annotated Ada 95 Reference Manual] states: "A shared passive package cannot contain library-level declarations of protected objects with entries, nor of task objects. Task objects are disallowed because passive partitions don't have any threads of control of their own, nor any run-time system of their own. Protected objects with entries are disallowed because an entry queue contains references to calling tasks, and that would require in effect a pointer from a passive partition back to a task in some active partition." The Distributed Systems Annex does not address synchronization issues on the data declared in a shared passive package.

The following example presented by [Volz et al., 1995] describes a simple distributed program. The program calculates and displays an image of a *Mandlebrot* set using three partitions:

- One partition to calculate the top half of the image,

- One partition to calculate the bottom half of the image, and

- One partition to display the image.

Each of the partitions is an active partition. As stated above, the interface to an active partition is specified by an RCI package. A main program is also needed and can be assigned to any one of the three partitions. A pure package is used to specify type information for the communication between partitions. In this program, the Mandelbrot calculation routine calls the display routine at the end of calculating each image. The declared pure package defines a type for the image line:

```
package Image_Types is
  pragma Pure; -- allows data types and constant used across partitions
  ...
  type ROW_TYPE is array( 1 .. Num_Rows) of PIXEL_COLOR;
end Image_Types;
```

The display RCI has two procedures: a startup procedure to create the display window and a procedure to display a line once it is calculated:

```
with Image_Types;
package Display is
  pragma Remote_Call_Interface;
  ...
  procedure plot_start;
  procedure plot_row( row_no : INTEGER; row : Image_Types.ROW_TYPE);
end Display;
```

The two RCI packages used to calculate the image are very similar to each other. The top half RCI is given below. It contains a single routine which starts the calculation process when it is called.

```
package Calc_Top is
  pragma Remote_Call_Interface;
  ...
  procedure calc_slice( ... Mandelbrot params ... );
end Calc_Top;

with Image_Types;
with Display;
package body Calc_Top is
  procedure Calc_Slice( ... ... Mandelbrot params ... ) is
  begin
    ...
    Display.plot_row(row_no,row);
    ...
  end Calc_Slice;
end Calc_Top;
```

The main program is used to signal the display partition to create the window and to start the two calculation routines.

```
with Display;
with Calc_Top;
with Calc_Bot;
procedure Mandle is
begin
  ...
  Display.plot_start;
  calc_top.calc_slice( ... Mandelbrot params ... );
  calc_bot.calc_slice( ... Mandelbrot params ... );
end Mandle;
```

This example shows that minimal changes are required to specify whether the program is targeted for distributed or nondistributed execution. Only the pragma Remote_Call_Interface identifies that the program is distributed.

3.2 The distributed protected object model

As seen above, the remote procedure call paradigm is the specified communication facility between partitions in Ada 95. The RPC is of high interest, but it has also been viewed as too restrictive by some authors [Dobbings, 1993] [Birman and Van Renesse,

1994]. [Bal, 1990] shows that broadcasting is a more appropriate model than RPC for the traveling salesperson problem and for many other distributed and parallel applications. [Gargaro et al., 1995] also points out that paradigms such as those supported by Linda or Orca may be more appropriate in programming certain distributed applications. In addition, the shared memory paradigm in Ada 95 only partially supports protected objects, since these objects are restricted to being entry-less [Annoted Ada 95 Reference Manual] [Kermarrec and Pautet, 1994]. Entry-less protected objects preclude conditional synchronization (i.e., a condition must be true before the object's operation is executed) and therefore restrict their use. For example, the distributed implementation of the traveling salesperson problem presented by [Bal, 1990] requires the different worker tasks to synchronize themselves on the protected objects on certain conditions. Only entries in a protected object can provide conditional synchronization, and the Distributed Systems Annex does not address synchronization on protected objects with entries. Therefore, using only the Distributed Systems Annex, it is more difficult to solve this problem; and consequently, a model supporting protected objects with entries is attractive.

In addition, the following points reinforce the need to fully support protected objects in a distributed environment. [Volz et al., 1994] suggests that protected objects could be used as a basis for distributed program in a massively parallel situation. Protected objects are very similar to the constructs of some distributed programming languages which provide conditional synchronization: the shared data objects [Bal, 1992] of Orca, the capsules [Gehani, 1993] of an extension of Concurrent C/C++, the classes of Distributed Eiffel [Gunaseelan and LeBlanc, 1992], and the DoPVM extension [Hartley and Sunderam, 1993] of PVM [Sunderam, 1990].

With this in mind and with the fact that the Distributed Systems Annex leaves an implementator freedom to add other paradigms, the next chapter investigates how to implement protected objects with entries in a distributed environment using some implementation techniques used by Orca such as replication and broadcasting. For a detailed description of Orca, refer to [Bal and Tanenbaum, 1988] [Bal, 1990] [Bal et al., 1990a] [Bal et al., 1990b] [Bal et al., 1992a] [Bal et al., 1992b] [Bal et al., 1992c] [Tanenbaum et al., 1992] [Bal and Athanasiu, 1994].

Chapter 4

Distributed Protected Objects

The previous chapter summarized the different approaches to distributing an Ada program and introduced a new model based on distributed protected objects. This chapter presents this model in detail. Since no Ada 95 compilers was available at the time of this study, the current implementation uses an Ada 83 compiler and a methodology described by [Ledru, 1995a] to translate protected objects.

The approach taken is based on pre-partitioning and is similar to the DIADEM [Atkinson et al., 1988] approach, and makes use of a pre-translator which generates distributed Ada code from the original source. Distributed units (i.e., tasks and protected objects) are grouped into virtual nodes. These virtual nodes communicate with each other through remote rendezvous and remote protected operation call (i.e., protected functions, protected procedures, and entries). Partitioning is expressed by a pragma which is placed immediately before a task or a protected object declaration and causes the declared entity to be placed on the virtual node named as a parameter in the pragma. Determining where the program's virtual nodes execute is performed during a post-compilation phase using a configuration file which contains the mapping between virtual and physical nodes.

The following sections review the pre-translator in detail. First, task translation and protected object translation are described. Secondly, the subsystem which supports communication among virtual nodes is described. Finally, an example is presented.

4.1 Transformation

As stated above, the approach makes use of a pre-translator which generates the source of the library units for each virtual node. Each of these library units includes part of the original source and calls to the communication subsystem. Each library unit of a virtual node is then compiled by an existing compiler and binded with the communication subsystem. Another approach would be to design a compiler and run-time system able to support distributed tasks and distributed protected objects. However, such approach is not flexible and would require developing of an entirely new compiler.

4.2 Restrictions and Assumptions

Several problems were encountered while distributing tasks due to imprecisions in the Ada Language Reference Manual and due to implementation difficulties. Therefore, the model presented in this thesis, as other models do, imposes several restrictions on distributed tasks. Other restrictions are also imposed due to the pre-translator approach and features not yet implemented. Not surprisingly, since protected objects and tasks have similar syntactic characteristics, the restrictions which apply to tasks also apply to protected objects. Most of these restrictions are similar to the restrictions imposed by the Shared Passive and RCI pragmas.

The restrictions imposed on tasks and protected objects are:

• References to shared variables: Virtual nodes are only allowed to communicate through remote rendezvous and remote protected operation call. They are not allowed to communicate through shared variables [Gehani, 1982] since this would require a form of distributed shared memory. Sharing of library units (e.g., packages) among virtual nodes is possible only if the entities within the units do not possess an internal state (e.g., types).

• Passing access type variables as arguments in remote rendezvous or in remote protected operation call: Access type variables are only meaningful within the address space of the process in which it is being used. Ada 83 does not provide any mechanisms to convert access variables to a stream of bytes as does Ada 95 with the *Read* and the *Write* attributes. Therefore, it is not possible to use access variables in remote rendezvous or in remote protected operation call.

• Passing limited type variables as arguments in remote rendezvous or in remote protected operation call: The assignment operation is not allowed for a limited type. This precludes marshalling and unmarshalling before transmission and reception of the data unless mechanisms to convert these data are provided.

• Passing tasks and protected objects as arguments in remote rendezvous or in remote protected operation call: Tasks and protected objects are also only meaningful within the address space of the process in which they are being used [Volz et al., 1989]. Therefore, it is not possible to use tasks and protected objects as arguments in remote rendezvous or in remote protected operation call.

• Conditional Entry Calls: As stated by [Volz et al., 1985], conditional entry calls are a source of confusion. While it has been argued that conditional entry calls should always fail due to network delays, another interpretation suggests that a conditional entry call only depends on the readiness of the called task or of the called object and does not depend on the time required to initiate the rendezvous or the protected object's entry. The model presented here assumes the second interpretation.

• Timed Entry Calls: Timed entry calls imply a notion of system wide time. This system wide time needs to be supported by the underlying operating system using mechanisms such as clock resynchronization and drift prevention. As these mechanisms are not usually supported, timed entry calls need to be avoided.

• Asynchronous Transfer of Control (ATC): If the *triggering statement* is a remote task's entry call and the *abortable part* completes first, an attempt should be made to abort the remote task. If the *triggering statement* is a remote protected object's entry call and the abortable part completes first, an attempt should be made to dequeue the entry call. If the abortable part includes any tasks' remote entry calls and the triggering statement completes first, an attempt should be made to abort these remote tasks. If the abortable part includes any protected objects' remote entry calls and the triggering statement completes first, an attempt should be made to dequeue these entry calls. [Giering and Baker, 1994] describes some implementations problems presented by ATC, some of which present greater difficulties in a distributed environment. The model currently does not support ATC.

• Task Termination Detection: Several problems occur to detect task termination since the termination of a master task must wait for the termination of any children tasks. In a distributed environment, the master task may have to check termination conditions on other processors [Volz et al., 1989]. Some algorithms overcome this problem [Helary et al., 1987]. The model currently does not support task termination.

• Access Type Tasks and Protected Objects: As the next section shows, tasks and protected objects are transformed by the pre-translator into packages. Transforming tasks and protected objects into packages creates several problems because packages cannot be elements of arrays or of records, do not support entry families, and are not units from which multiple instances can be generated. The last problem is overcome by generic packages. But since generic packages can only be instantiated at compile time, this precludes access type translation.

4.3 Tasks

As a unit for expressing concurrency in a program, a task seems to be an ideal candidate for parallel distributed programming. Distributed tasks synchronize and communicate by means of a *remote rendezvous*. A remote rendezvous is a rendezvous among tasks located on different virtual nodes.

In a single machine environment, a task issuing an entry call and a task accepting this entry call establish a rendezvous. The two tasks communicate with each other during the rendezvous. In a distributed environment, where the task accepting the entry call is actually remote, this entry becomes a *remote entry*. Since the callee task is located on a remote machine, a different version of the entry called a *client stub* is made visible to the caller task. The purpose of the client stub is to pack the parameters of the entry into a message and to send this message to the remote task. When the message arrives at the remote task, it is received by a *server stub*. The client stub and the server stub communicate with each other through the communication subsystem.

When a caller issues an entry call, the parameters of the original call become parameters of the remote entry call and are marshalled into a message which also includes a parameter identifying the called entry. One formal *in* parameter is added to the remote entry call to indicate the type of the call (normal or conditional). The client stub then sends the message to the server stub, awaits a reply message, unmarshalls it, and passes the parameters to the application; a timeout exception or a tasking error exception is raised by the remote entry call if the reply message includes failure or timeout status.

On the remote task side, the server stub provides a dispatcher waiting for messages. When a message is received by the dispatcher, it is unmarshalled and interpreted in order to select the appropriate entry, then passed on to a local agent task to prevent serialization. The dispatcher then loops back to repeat this process for subsequent messages. The local agent task issues the actual entry call, receives the *out* parameters from the rendezvous, marshalls these parameters, sends back a reply message to the caller, and then terminates.

Since the model presented in this thesis is restricted to using an existing compiler, modifications to this compiler to support distributed tasks are not possible. Therefore, distributed tasks are transformed by the pre-translator into appropriate constructs to include client stubs and server stubs.

On the client side, a task is replaced by a package, and each entry is replaced by a procedure. When a caller issues an entry call such as "task_name.entry_name", this entry call becomes "package_name.procedure_name".

The following example illustrates the transformation of a task into a package. The task Service defined as remote by the pragma distributed is transformed into the package Service, while its entry Request is transformed into the procedure Request. The *in* parameters of the procedure are marshalled and transferred over the network to the server stub using the procedure Trans provided by the communication subsystem. The procedure Trans blocks, waiting for a reply from the server. Once a reply is available, it is unmarshalled, and the *out* parameters are passed to the application:

Inter-Task Communication (Original code)
```
pragma distributed( Node => Node_1);
task Service is
  entry Request( I : in INTEGER; C : out CHARACTER);
end Service;
```

Client Stub (Translated code)
```
with Control_Types;
package Service is ...
package body Service is -- Client Stub
  procedure Service
    ( The_Call      : in Control_Types.CALL_TASK := Control_Types.CALLABLE;
      The_Response : in out Control_Types.RESPONSE_TASK ) is ...

  procedure Request
    ( I          : in INTEGER;
      C          : out CHARACTER;
      The_Call  : in Control_Types.CALL_ENTRY := Control_Types.NORMAL ) is
    The_In_Msg  : Service_Types.Service_CALL_GLOBAL_MSG;
    The_Out_Msg : Service_Types.Service_RESPONSE_GLOBAL_MSG;
  begin -- Request
    -- marshalling of in and in out parameters
    The_In_Msg := ...
    Communication.Trans( ... );
    if ( The_Out_Message.The_Response = Control_Types.FAILURE) then
      raise Tasking_Error;
    elsif ( The_Out_Message.The_Response = Control_Types.TIMED_OUT) then
      raise Time_Out;
    -- unmarshalling of in out and out parameters
  exception
    when Communication_Error =>
      raise Tasking_Error;
  end Request;
end Service;
```

A conditional entry call is replaced by a *block* statement with an exception handler catching the timeout exception and executing the appropriate sequence of statements. The following example illustrates this transformation:

Conditional entry call original code:
```
select
  Controller.Request(Some_Item);
else
  Try_Something_Else;
end select;
```

Conditional entry call translated code:
```
begin
  Controller.Request(Some_Item, Control_Types.CONDITIONAL);
exception
  when Controller.Time_Out => Try_Something_Else;
end;
```

A request to abort a remote task and to test whether a task is callable or terminated is replaced by a call to an additional procedure introduced in the package replacing the original task. The following example illustrates this transformation:

Callable attribute test original code:
```
if Task_X'CALLABLE then
  Text_IO.Put_Line("Task_X is callable");
end if;
```

Callable attribute translated code:
```
Task_X.Task_X( Control_Types.CALLABLE, The_Response);
if The_Response = CALLABLE then
  Text_IO.Put_Line("Task_X is callable");
end if;
```

On the server side, a task is replaced by a package encapsulating a dispatcher to receive the messages, a local agent task for each entry, and the original task. The following example illustrates the transformation of a task into a package. The task body `Service` is transformed into the package body `Service`. The task `Dispatcher` waits for an incoming message and creates an appropriate local agent task once a message is available, either `Process_Service_Task_Type` or `Process_Service_Request_Type`, then waits for another message. `Process_Service_Task_Type` issues the operation, sends back a reply to the caller, and then terminates. `Process_Service_Request_Type` calls the entry

`Request` of the task `Service`, receives the out parameters from the rendezvous, marshalls these parameters, send back a reply to the client stub, and then terminates.

Inter-Task Communication (Original code)

```
task body Service is
begin -- Service
  -- ...
  accept Request( I : in INTEGER; C : out CHARACTER) do
    -- process request
  end Request;
  -- ...
end Service;
```

Server Stub (Translated code)

```
package body Service_Tasks is -- Server Stub
  task Dispatcher is
    entry Start;
  end Dispatcher;

  -- Local Agent for the task
  task type Process_Service_Task_Type is
    entry Start( The_Msg : Service_Types.Service_CALL_MSG);
  end Process_Service_Task_Type;
  type Process_Service_Task is access Process_Service_Task_Type;
  -- Local Agent for entry request
  task type Process_Service_Request_Type is
    entry Start( The_Msg : Service_Types.Service_Request_CALL_MSG);
  end Process_Service_Request_Type;
  type Process_Service_Request
    is access Process_Service_Request_Type;

  task body Service is
  begin -- Service
    -- ...
    accept Request( I : in INTEGER; C : out CHARACTER) do
      -- process request
    end Request;
    -- ...
  end Service;

  task body Process_Service_Task_Type is
    The_In_Msg  : Service_Types.Service_CALL_MSG;
    The_Out_Msg : Service_Types.Service_RESPONSE_MSG;
  begin -- Process_Service_Task_Type
    accept Start( The_Msg : Service_Types.Service_CALL_MSG ) do
      The_In_Msg := The_Msg;
    end Start;
    case The_Msg.The_Call is
      when Control_Types.ABORT_T =>
        -- process request, send back reply
      when Control_Types.CALLABLE =>
        -- process request, send back reply
```

```
      when Control_Types.TERMINATED =>
         -- process request, send back reply
    end case;
  end Process_Service_Task_Type;

  task body Process_Service_Request_Type is
    The_In_Msg  : Service_Types.Service_Request_CALL_MSG;
    The_Out_Msg : Service_Types.Service_Request_RESPONSE_MSG;
  begin -- Process_Service_Request_Type
    accept Start( The_Msg : Service_Types.Service_Request_CALL_MSG ) do
      The_In_Msg := The_Msg;
    end;
    case The_In_Msg.The_Call is
      when Control_Types.NORMAL =>
        begin
          -- call the entry request
          Service.Request(The_In_Msg.I, The_Out_Msg.C);
          The_Out_Msg.The_Response := Control_Types.SUCCESS;
          -- local agent sends back reply and terminates
          Communication.Send( ... );
        exception
          when others =>
            The_Out_Msg.The_Response := Control_Types.FAILURE;
            Communication.Send( ... );
        end;
      when Control_Types.CONDITIONAL =>
        ...
    end case;
  end Process_Service_Request_Type;

  task Dispatcher is
  begin -- Dispatcher
    loop -- forever
      Communication.Recv( ... );
      case The_In_Msg.The_Mode is
        when Service_Types.Service_CALL =>
          -- create a new local agent to process operation
          The_Process_Service_Task := new Process_Service_Task_Type;
          The_Process_Service_Task.Start(The_In_Msg.Service);
        when Service_Types.Service_Request_CALL =>
          -- create a new local agent to call the entry request
          The_Process_Service_Request_Type;
             := new Process_Service_Request_Type;
          The_Process_Service_Request.Start(The_In_Msg.Service_Request);
      end case;
    end loop;
  end Dispatcher;
end Service_Tasks;
```

Figure 4.1 recapitulates the control flow among the different components of a remote rendezvous.

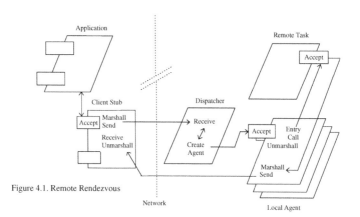

Figure 4.1. Remote Rendezvous

4.4 Protected Objects

Although protected objects are intended for shared-memory systems, [Bal, 1995] suggests that since protected objects are very similar to the shared data objects of the Orca language, it should be possible to implement them efficiently not only on multiprocessors but also on distributed systems. This section reviews how protected objects can be implemented on distributed systems using some implementation techniques used by Orca. For a detailed comparison between Orca's shared data objects and Ada's protected objects, refer to [Bal, 1995].

Chapter 2 discussed several implementations for the shared data objects in Orca. Likewise, similar implementations for the protected objects in Ada are possible.

The implementation described here is based on total replication of the protected objects since it is efficient, is relatively easy to implement, and uses the update protocol described in Chapter 2.

In a single machine environment, protected objects ensure mutual exclusion to data shared by several tasks of a given process. In a distributed environment, protected objects ensure mutual exclusion to data shared by several tasks of several virtual nodes. Using a replication scheme, each protected object is replicated on each virtual node. Each object is accessed by all tasks running on that virtual node via functions, procedures, or entries. Functions (which do not modify the state of the object) use the object directly. Procedures and entries (which do modify the state of the object) broadcast the operation to be performed and its parameters to all replicated protected objects to ensure that all the objects are updated simultaneously. Since procedures and entries modify the state of the object, all replicated objects must be ensured to receive messages in the same order. To do so, procedures and entries first send a point-to-point message to a sequencer which then broadcasts the message. Figure 4.2 recapitulates the control flow between the different components of a remote protected procedure call or of a remote entry call.

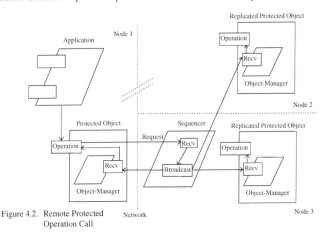

Figure 4.2. Remote Protected Operation Call

Since the model presented in this thesis is restricted to using an existing compiler, modifications to this compiler to support distributed protected objects are not possible.

Therefore, protected objects are transformed by the pre-translator into appropriate constructs to support their distribution. In order to ensure the serialization of the access to the protected object, a sequencer is created for each protected object. This sequencer is implemented by a package. Also, the protected object itself is replaced by a package; each entry is replaced by a procedure while functions and procedures stay unchanged. An *object-manager* task is added into each package to handle messages from the sequencer. A procedure or an entry sending a message to its sequencer suspends until the message has been received back, then continues. When a remote message is received by an object-manager, it is unmarshalled and interpreted in order to select the appropriate procedure or entry, then executed immediately to ensure serialization. Procedures and entries whose barrier condition is true are executed immediately within the object-manager since operations are expected to execute in a short amount of time; entries of which barrier condition is false are executed by a task spawned by the object-manager. The object-manager only resumes its execution once the task has been queued on the object entry to prevent race conditions. Operations are executed by all object-managers in the same order but not necessarily at the same time. If a function is currently executed by a given task, a remote procedure or a remote entry will have to wait until the function terminates. Nevertheless, this is still in agreement with the serialization principle.

The following example illustrates the actions performed by an object-manager. When a message is received (`recv message`), the object-manager checks whether the message originates from the current virtual node or not (`Msg.The_Node = Current_Node`). If so, the current task is unlocked (`unlock current task`). Otherwise, the operation is executed (`execute operation`):

```
task body Object_Manager is
begin -- Object_Manager
  loop
    recv message;
    if Msg.The_Node = Current_Node then
      unlock current task;
    else
      identify operation to perform;
```

```
      execute operation;
    end if;
  end loop;
end Object_Manager;
```

A protected object is transformed into two packages. The following example illustrates the transformation of a protected object with three operations: a function to return the current value of the counter, a procedure to increment the value of the counter, and an entry to decrement the value of the counter if this value is positive. The protected object Counter defined as remote by the pragma distributed is transformed into a package to support the sequencer and a package to support the object itself. An example of the sequencer follows. The package specification keeps the procedure Increment and the function Value_Of unchanged while the entry Decrement is replaced by a procedure with an additional parameter to specify the type of call. An exception is added to handle conditional entry calls. The package body includes a dispatcher (Handle) to receive messages from the sequencer, a local agent task for the entry Decrement, and the original operations:

Protected Counter (Original code)

```
pragma distributed( Node => Node_0);
protected Counter is
  procedure Increment( New_Value : out NATURAL);
  entry Decrement( New_Value : out NATURAL);
  -- barrier condition: when Data > 0
  function Value_Of return NATURAL;
private
  Data : NATURAL := 0;
end Counter;
```

Protected Counter (Translated code)

```
package Counter is
  timeout : exception; -- raised by conditional entry calls
  procedure Increment( New_Value : out NATURAL);
  procedure Decrement
    ( New_Value : out NATURAL;
      The_Call  : in CALL_ENTRY := NORMAL);
  function Value_Of return NATURAL;

private
  Data : NATURAL := 0;
end Counter;
package body Counter is
  ...
```

```
-- Object manager
task Handle is
  entry Start;
end Handle;

-- Local agent task
type Decrement_Task_Type;
type Decrement_Task is access Decrement_Task_Type;
task Decrement_Task_Type is
  entry Start
    ( The_Call_Msg  : in CALL_ENTRY;
      The_Task_Msg  : in Decrement_Task );
end Decrement_Task_Type;

task body Handle is
begin -- Handle
  accept Start ...
  loop
    Communication.Recv( ... );
    Semaphore.Wait(Handler_Lock);
    if The_Msg.The_Node = Get_Node
      Semaphore.Release(Distributed_Lock);
    else
      case The_Msg.The_Operation is
        ...
      end case;
    end if;
    Semaphore.Release(Handler_Lock);
  end loop;
end Handle;

procedure Increment ...
procedure Decrement ...
function Value_Of ...

end Counter;
```

The sequencer (Counter_Sequencer_Task) is composed of one task (Handle_Msg) waiting for messages from the objects. The task consists of an infinite loop with each iteration of the loop handling one message. Depending on applications, one task may call the sequencer more than others. In order to minimize overall communication overhead, it is best to place the task calling the sequencer the most in the virtual node where the sequencer resides. The parameter (Node => Node_0) of the pragma distributed provides the programmer with capability of specifying the location of the sequencer. Communication between an object and its sequencer and between a sequencer and the replicated objects is carried out by the communication subsystem.

Sequencer (Translated code)

```
package Counter_Sequencer_Task is
  task Handle_Msg is
    entry Start;
  end Handle_Msg;
end Counter_Sequencer_Task;

package body Counter_Sequencer_Task is
  task body Handle_Msg is
  begin -- Handle_Msg
    accept Start;
    loop
      Communication.Recv(...);
      Communication.Broadcast(...);
    end loop;
  end Handle_Msg;
end Counter_Sequencer_Task;
```

4.4.1 Protected Functions

Functions are for read-only accesses, and therefore if a task is executing a function, any other task can access the same protected object only via functions. Also, functions do not require distributed operations (i.e., broadcasting the operation to other virtual nodes) since they do not modify the state of the protected object and therefore can be executed locally.

A function is transformed into two functions, one to perform the original operation, and the other to implement the locking mechanism which prevents procedures and entries from modifying the protected data while a function is being executed.

The following example illustrates the transformation of a function. The original function (Value_Of) is renamed to Value_Of_internal. A new function (Value_Of) implements the locking mechanism. The *object mutual exclusion lock* (Lock) is seized by the first function entering the protected object and released by the last function leaving the protected object. The semaphore P ensures that only one function at a time will increment and decrement the number of functions currently being executed. If any exception occurs in the original function, the number of functions being executed is decremented, and the semaphore Lock is released if necessary:

Function (Original code)

```
function Value_Of return NATURAL is
begin -- Value_Of_internal
```

```
  return Data;
end Value_Of;
```

Function (Translated code)
```
function Value_Of_internal return NATURAL is
begin -- Value_Of_internal
  return Data;
end Value_Of_internal;
function Value_Of return NATURAL is
  Temp : NATURAL;
begin -- Value_Of
  Semaphore.Wait(P);
  C := C + 1;
  if (C = 1) then
    Semaphore.Wait(Lock);
  end if;
  Semaphore.Release(P);
  Temp := Value_Of_internal;
  Semaphore.Wait(P);
  C := C - 1;
  if (C = 0) then
    Semaphore.Release(Lock);
  end if;
  Semaphore.Release(P);
  return Temp;
exception
  when others =>
    Semaphore.Wait(P);
    C := C - 1;
    if (C = 0) then
      Semaphore.Release(Lock);
    end if;
    Semaphore.Release(P);
end Value_Of;
```

4.4.2 Protected Procedures

Procedures are for read-write accesses, and therefore if a task is accessing protected data via a procedure, any other accesses to the protected object are excluded. Procedures modify the state of the protected object, and thus the state of all replicated objects must be updated accordingly.

Protected procedures are transformed into three parts. The first part is to perform the intended operations of the procedures and is decomposed into three procedures: the first performs the original operation, the second provides the locking mechanism which prevents other operations from accessing the protected data while a procedure is being executed, and the third broadcasts the operation to be executed to other virtual nodes so that the replicated data can also be updated. The second part of the transformed protected procedures is a task called object-manager which is responsible for receiving broadcasted messages for all the procedures and entries. The third part is a procedure whose purpose is to evaluate the entry barriers for all the entries once the protected data have been modified.

When a task calls a protected procedure, the procedure first sends the message to its sequencer discussed previously. The sequencer in turn broadcasts the message to all the virtual nodes including the one which initiated the message. Meanwhile, the procedure which sent the message to the sequencer suspends until the message is received back by its object manager. Once the object manager receives the message, it allows the procedure to continue. A message which an object-manager receives can either originate from the same object, or originate from a replicated object. In the former case, the object-manager unlocks the procedure by releasing a lock, and in the latter case, the object-manager executes the operation to update the replicated object. The operation first acquires the mutual exclusion lock on the object, executes the original procedure, and evaluates the entry barriers. Depending on the entry barriers, the operation may release the mutual exclusion lock.

As previously mentioned, in Ada a protected procedure cannot call any blocking operations (e.g., entries), and therefore an advanced scheme such as the one described by [Bal et al., 1992a] is not necessary. Even though a procedure cannot call any entries, it may call other non-blocking protected operations such as protected procedures and protected functions. When a protected subprogram is executed it acquires a mutual exclusion lock. So, when a called protected subprogram is within the same protected object as a caller protected procedure, the callee will try to acquire the mutual exclusion lock which is already held by the caller. Thus this causes a deadlock. In order to resolve this problem, a call on a protected subprogram within the same protected object should not start a new protected action but is considered to be a part of the current action.

Another problem occurs when a called protected subprogram is not within the same protected object as a caller protected procedure. Since protected functions are read-only, a call on a function does not require special processing and is considered as a regular function call. But when a protected procedure is called, it broadcasts the operation to perform. When a protected procedure A calls an external protected procedure B, all the duplicates of A will also call B. It is necessary to prevent multiple copies of B from broadcasting. In order to resolve this problem, only one copy of procedure B broadcasts the operation to perform while the other copies of B suspend their execution until receiving the broadcast message.

The following example illustrates the transformation of a procedure. The original procedure (Increment) is renamed to Increment_internal. Two new procedures (Increment_Local and Increment) are added in the package body along with an object-manager (Handle) which receives messages from the sequencer. Note that one object-manager is created for all the procedures and entries to be transformed. In this example, the explanation of the procedure which evaluates the entry barriers is omitted. It is discussed in the next section in more detail. When a task calls the procedure Increment, the procedure first marshalls the *in* parameters in a message and acquires a semaphore Temp_Lock. The semaphore Temp_Lock prevents any other task in the same virtual node from sending a message before the task which called the procedure Increment first has received its message back. The sequencer serializes messages among virtual nodes, and the lock Temp_Lock does the same among tasks in a virtual node. The procedure then sends a message to the sequencer and blocks on the semaphore Distributed_Lock until it is released by the object-manager, and then calls the procedure Increment_Local. When the object-manager Handle receives a message, it releases the lock Distributed_Lock if the message originated from the same virtual node, or calls the procedure Increment_Local otherwise. The procedure Increment_Local first seizes the lock (Lock) which ensures mutually exclusive access to the object. Once Lock is acquired, the procedure releases the semaphore Temp_Lock in order to allow other tasks in the original virtual node to initiate a protected operation call, and calls the renamed original procedure (Increment_internal). Finally, the procedure Increment_Local checks whether any barrier conditions need to be reevaluated (Evaluate_Entry_Barrier), and based on the barrier conditions, the lock (Lock) is released.

Procedure (Original code)

```
procedure Increment( New_Value : out NATURAL) is
begin -- Increment
  Data := Data + 1;
  New_Value := Data;
end Increment;
```

Procedure (Translated code)

```
procedure Increment_internal( New_Value : out NATURAL) is
begin -- Increment_internal
  Data := Data + 1;
  New_Value := Data;
end Increment_internal;
procedure Increment_Local( New_Value : out NATURAL; The_Node : NODE) is
begin -- Increment_Local
  Semaphore.Wait(Lock);
  if The_Node = Get_Node then
    Semaphore.Release(Temp_Lock);
  end if;
  Increment_internal( New_Value );
  Evaluate_Entry_Barrier;
exception
  when others =>
    Evaluate_Entry_Barrier;
    raise;
end Increment_Local;

task body Handle is
begin -- Handle
  loop
    Communication.Recv(...);
    if The_Msg.The_Node = Get_Node then
      Semaphore.Release(Distributed_Lock);
    else
      case The_Msg.The_Operation is
        when Counter_Types.Increment =>
          declare
            New_Value : NATURAL;
          begin
            Increment_Local(New_Value, The_Msg.The_Node);
          end;
        when Counter_Types.Decrement =>
          ...
```

```
   end case;
  end if;
 end loop;
end Handle;

procedure Increment ( New_Value : out NATURAL) is
begin -- Increment
 The_Msg := ...
 Semaphore.Wait(Temp_Lock);
 Communication.Send(...);
 Semaphore.Wait(Distributed_Lock);
 Increment_Local(New_Value, The_Msg.The_Node);
end Increment;
```

4.4.3 Entries

Like procedures, entries are for read-write accesses, but in addition, they specify a barrier condition which must be true before the call is allowed to proceed. Like procedures, entries modify the state of the protected object, and therefore the state of all replicated objects must be updated. But entries differ from procedures in that an entry call may be cancelled if it is not selected immediately (conditional entry calls) or before an expiration time is reached (timed entry calls). As previously mentioned, timed entry calls, however, are not addressed in a distributed environment.

Entries are transformed into three parts. One to perform the intended operations of the entries, and the other two are similar to those for the procedures, i.e., the object-manager and the procedure to evaluate the entry barriers. In order to perform the intended operations for entries, each original entry is transformed into four procedures and one task. The first procedure is to perform the original operation, the second to provide the locking and barrier testing mechanism for procedures originating the call, the third to provide the locking and barrier testing mechanism for replicated procedures, and the last to broadcast the operation to be executed to other virtual nodes. The task created is called the *local agent* task, and it is to perform entries whose barrier condition is false.

When a task calls an entry, the entry first sends a message to its sequencer, then suspends until the message has been received by the object-manager. The object-manager receives a message originating from either the same object or a replicated object.

In the former case, the object-manager unlocks the task executing the entry which then evaluates the entry barrier, and executes the entry if the barrier condition is true or blocks on a semaphore otherwise. If the barrier condition is false and the call is conditional, the call returns immediately. If the call is unconditional, the following occurs. In order to simulate the entry queue, a semaphore is created and added to the entry queue. The Count attribute of the entry, which denotes the number of tasks waiting on the entry queue, is incremented. The barrier condition of each entry is reevaluated since a task which had been queued on a false barrier may be able to proceed due to the change in the Count attribute of the current entry. The execution of the entry body is suspended. Once the entry body resumes its execution, the Count attribute is decremented, the protected action is performed, and finally the barrier condition of each entry is reevaluated one more time. 'In the latter case, the object-manager evaluates the entry barrier and executes the entry if the barrier condition is true; otherwise, it spawns a local agent task which is added to the entry queue. The function of the local agent task is to execute the entry since the object manager cannot block. If the barrier condition is false and the call is conditional, the call returns immediately. If the call is unconditional, the following occurs. The local agent task increments the Count attribute of the entry, reevaluates the barrier condition of each entry, waits on a rendezvous, decrements the Count attribute once the rendezvous is accepted, performs the protected action, and finally reevaluates the barrier condition of each entry.

The procedure which evaluates the entry barriers is called whenever an entry call is queued and an entry (or a procedure) terminates. The procedure tests if any entry waiting in a queue has a true barrier condition, in which case the entry is allowed to resume its execution. If none of the barrier conditions are true, the object mutual exclusion lock is released, and an external task can access the protected object. The procedure must ensure that all entries are unlocked in the same order, whether they are waiting on a semaphore or on a local agent task's *accept statement*; this is achieved by a FIFO queue of variant records whose alternatives are either semaphores or local agent tasks. The object issuing the request waits on a semaphore while the replicated objects wait on accept statements. As previously mentioned, in Ada an entry barrier is not allowed to depend on its parameters. So the procedure does not test individual callers of an entry. This rule ensures that all callers of the same entry see the same barrier condition, allowing the barrier to be checked without examining individual callers. Without this rule, as in Orca, each caller of a given entry would have to be treated separately since each might have a different effective barrier value.

The following example illustrates the transformation of an entry. The original entry (Decrement) is renamed to the procedure Decrement_internal. Three new procedures (Decrement_Local, Decrement_Remote, and Decrement) and a task (Decrement_Task_Type) are added in the package body. As mentioned before, an object-manager task (Handle) and a procedure which evaluates the entry barriers (Evaluate_Entry_Barrier) are also added in the package body. When a task calls the procedure Decrement, the procedure first marshalls the *in* parameters in a message and acquires a semaphore Temp_Lock, as explained in the previous section. The procedure then sends a message to the sequencer and blocks on the semaphore Distributed_Lock until it is released by the object-manager, and then calls the procedure Decrement_Local. The procedure Decrement_Local first seizes the lock (Lock) which ensures mutually exclusive access to the object, then evaluates its entry barrier. If the entry barrier condition (Decrement_barrier) is true, the procedure Decrement_internal is executed immediately. If the entry barrier condition is false and the call is conditional, the call returns immediately. If the call is unconditional, the Count attribute of the entry is incremented, the barrier condition of each entry is reevaluated (Evaluate_Entry_Barrier), and a semaphore (Lock_On_Decrement) which is added to the entry queue is created. Once the semaphore is released within Evaluate_Entry_Barrier, the Count attribute is decremented and the procedure Decrement_internal is executed. When the object-manager Handle receives a message, it releases the lock Distributed_Lock if the message originated from the same virtual node, or calls the procedure Decrement_Remote otherwise. The procedure Decrement_Remote first seizes the lock (Lock). Once Lock is acquired, the procedure evaluates its entry barrier. If the entry barrier condition is true, the procedure Decrement_internal is executed immediately. If the entry barrier condition is false and the call is conditional, the call returns immediately. If the call is unconditional, a local agent task (Decrement_Task_Type) which is added to the entry queue is created dynamically. The task first increments the Count attribute, reevaluates the entry barrier of each entry, then blocks on an accept statement. Once the procedure Evaluate_Entry_Barrier rendezvouses with the task, the Count attribute is decremented and the procedure Decrement_internal is executed.

<u>Entry (Original code)</u>

```
entry Decrement( New_Value : out NATURAL) when Data > 0 is
begin -- Decrement
  Data := Data - 1;
  New_Value := Data;
end Decrement;
```

<u>Entry (Translated code)</u>

```
procedure Decrement_internal
  ( New_Value : out NATURAL) is
begin -- Decrement_internal
  Data := Data - 1;
  New_Value := Data;
end Decrement_internal;

procedure Decrement_Local
  ( New_Value : out NATURAL;
    The_Call  : in CALL_ENTRY := NORMAL) is
  ...
begin -- Decrement_Local
  Semaphore.Wait(Lock);
  Semaphore.Release(Temp_Lock);
  if not ( Decrement_barrier ) then
    if the_Call = CONDITIONAL then
      raise Time_Out;
    end if;
    Lock_On_Decrement := Semaphore.CreateMutex;
    Semaphore.Wait(Lock_On_Decrement);
    Decrement_Lock_Queue.Add
      ( The_Item     => ( Local, Lock_On_Decrement),
        To_The_Queue => The_Decrement_Queue );
```

```
      Decrement_Count := Decrement_Count + 1;
      Evaluate_Entry_Barrier;
      Semaphore.Wait(Lock_On_Decrement);
      Semaphore.Close(Lock_On_Decrement);
      Decrement_Count := Decrement_Count - 1;
    end if;
  Decrement_internal(New_Value);
  Evaluate_Entry_Barrier;
exception
  when Time_Out =>
    Evaluate_Entry_Barrier;
    raise Time_Out;
  when others =>
    ...
end Decrement_Local;

procedure Decrement_Remote
  ( New_Value : out NATURAL;
    The_Call  : in CALL_ENTRY := NORMAL) is
  The_Decrement_Task : Decrement_Task;
begin -- Decrement_Remote
  Semaphore.Wait(Lock);
  if not (Decrement_Barrier) then
    if The_Call = CONDITIONAL then
      raise Time_Out;
    end if;
    The_Decrement_Task := new Decrement_Task_Type;
    Decrement_Lock_Queue.Add
      ( The_Item      => (Remote, The_Decrement_Task),
        To_The_Queue => The_Decrement_Queue );
    The_Decrement_Task.Start( The_Decrement_Task);
  else
    Decrement_internal(New_Value);
    Evaluate_Entry_Barrier;
  end if;
exception
  ...
end Decrement_Remote;

-- local agent task
task body Decrement_Task_Type is
  ...
begin -- Decrement_Task_Type
  accept Start
    ( The_Task_Msg : in Decrement_Task ) do
    The_Task   := The_Task_Msg;
  end Start;
  Decrement_Count := Decrement_Count + 1;
  Evaluate_Entry_Barrier;
  accept Unlock;
  Decrement_Count := Decrement_Count - 1;
  Decrement_internal( New_Value );
  Evaluate_Entry_Barrier;
```

```
exception
  when others =>
    ...
end Decrement_Task_Type;

procedure Evaluate_Entry_Barrier is
begin -- Evaluate_Entry_Barrier
  if ( ( Decrement_barrier ) and ( Decrement_Count /= 0 ) ) then
    case Decrement_Lock_Queue.Front_Of
      ( The_Queue => The_Decrement_Queue ).The_Location is
      when Local =>
        Semaphore.Release(Decrement_Lock_Queue.Front_Of
          ( The_Queue => The_Decrement_Queue ).The_Semaphore );
      when Remote =>
        Decrement_Lock_Queue.Front_Of
          ( The_Queue => The_Decrement_Queue ).The_Task.Unlock;
    end case;
    Decrement_Lock_Queue.Pop(The_Queue => The_Decrement_Queue);
  elsif
    test other entries
  else
    -- allow an external call
    Semaphore.Release(Lock);
  end if;
end Evaluate_Entry_Barrier;

task body Handle is
begin -- Handle
  loop
    Communication.Recv(...);
    if The_Msg.The_Node = Get_Node then
      Semaphore.Release(Distributed_Lock);
    else
      case The_Msg.The_Operation is
        when Counter_Types.Increment =>
          ...
        when Counter_Types.Decrement =>
          declare
            New_Value : NATURAL;
          begin
            Decrement_Remote(New_Value, The_Msg.The_Call);
          end;
      end case;
    end if;
  end loop;
end Handle;

procedure Decrement
  ( New_Value : out NATURAL;
    The_Call  : in CALL_ENTRY := NORMAL) is
begin -- Decrement
  The_Msg := ...
  Semaphore.Wait(Temp_Lock);
```

```
 Communication.Send(...);
 Semaphore.Wait(Distributed_Lock);
 Decrement_Local(New_Value);
end Decrement;
```

4.4.4 Requeue Statement

As stated previously, an entry is not always executed atomically; i.e., it may include intermediate blockings as part of a requeue statement. A requeue statement is used to end an entry body while redirecting the corresponding entry call to a new entry call.

The syntax of the requeue statement may be specified as *with abort*. In this case, when the original entry call is aborted, the requeued call is cancelled, and no action is performed. If the original entry call was conditional and the barrier condition of the requeued call is false, the requeued call returns immediately. If the requeue statement is not specified as *with abort*, the requeued call remains protected despite cancellation of the original entry call.

As mentioned in the previous section, entries are transformed into procedures. Consequently, requeue statements are handled similar to protected procedures called by other protected procedures. When an entry is requeued on another entry, the requeue statement is replaced by a *requeue block*. The requeue block first checks the state of the barrier of the requeued procedure. If the barrier condition is true, the requeued procedure is executed immediately. Since the requeue statement is implemented as a procedure call, the requeued call returns while the requeued entry does not. So, a *requeue exception* is used to avoid executing the statements following the requeue in the caller procedure. If the barrier condition of the requeued procedure is false and the original call is conditional, the requeued call returns immediately. If the original call is unconditional, the following occurs. The requeued procedure is part of an action originating from either the same object or a replicated object. In the former case a semaphore suspends the task, while in the latter case a local agent task performs the protected action. Also, the requeued procedure is either within the same object as the caller procedure (internal requeue), or outside the object (external requeue). As discussed in section 4.4.2, if it is an internal requeue, the call is added by each replicated object to the queue of the requeued procedure. If it is an external requeue, the call is broadcasted by one of the objects, and the others suspend their execution until receiving the broadcast message.

The following example illustrates the transformation of an internal *requeue with abort*. The original requeue statement (`requeue Reset with abort`) is replaced by a requeue block. The requeue block first tests the barrier condition of the requeued procedure (`Reset_barrier`). If the barrier condition is true, the requeued procedure (`Reset_internal`) is executed immediately, and the exception `requeue` is raised when the procedure returns. If the barrier condition of `Reset_internal` is false and the call to `Signal_internal` is conditional, the call returns immediately since the requeue is specified as *with abort*. If the barrier condition is false, a semaphore (`Lock_On_Reset`) suspends the task, or a local agent task (`The_Reset_Task`) performs the protected action (`Reset_internal`).

Requeue Statement (Original code)

```
entry Signal when TRUE is
begin -- Signal
  if X > 0 then
    Occured := TRUE;
    requeue Reset with abort;
  end if;
end Signal;
entry Reset when X = 0 is
begin -- Reset
  Occured := FALSE;
end Reset;
```

Requeue Statement (Translated code)

```
procedure Signal_internal
  ( The_Node  : in Node.NODE;
    The_Call  : in CALL_ENTRY) is
begin -- Signal_internal
  if X > 0 then
    Occured := TRUE;
    -- requeue block
    if not (Reset_barrier) then
      if The_Call = CONDITIONAL then
        raise Time_Out;
      end if;
      if The_Node = Get_Node then
        declare
          Lock_On_Reset : Semaphore.MUTEX;
        begin
          Lock_On_Reset := Semaphore.CreateMutex;
          Semaphore.Wait(Lock_On_Reset);
          Reset_Lock_Queue.Add
            ( The_Item     => (Local, Lock_On_Reset),
              To_The_Queue => The_Reset_Queue );
          Reset_Count := Reset_Count + 1;
          Evaluate_Entry_Barrier;
          Semaphore.Wait(Lock_On_Reset);
          Semaphore.Close(Lock_On_Reset);
          Reset_Count := Reset_Count - 1;
        end;
      else -- Node /= Get_Node
        declare
          The_Reset_Task := new Reset_Task_Type;
        begin
          Reset_Lock_Queue.Add
            ( The_Item     => ( Remote, The_Reset_Task),
              To_The_Queue => The_Reset_Queue );
          The_Reset_Task.Start( The_Reset_Task );
          raise requeue;
        end;
      end if;
      Reset_internal;
      raise requeue;
    end if;
  end if;
end Signal_internal;
procedure Reset_internal is
begin -- Reset_internal
  Occured := FALSE;
end Reset_internal;

task body Reset_Task_Type is
begin --Reset_Task_Type
  accept Start
    ( The_Task_Msg : in Decrement_Task ) do
    The_Task  := The_Task_Msg;
```

```
  end Start;
  Reset_Count := Reset_Count + 1;
  Evaluate_Entry_Barrier;
  accept Unlock;
  Reset_Count := Reset_Count - 1;
  Reset_internal;
  Evaluate_Entry_Barrier;
exception
  when others =>
    ...
end Reset_Task_Type;
```

4.5 Communication Subsystem

The communication subsystem is composed of two parts. The first is a daemon that resides on all the computers making up the virtual machine. A user wishing to execute a distributed program configures a virtual machine by specifying the mapping between virtual nodes and physical nodes; only the daemons listed in the mapping file are used by the application. The second part of the system is a library of communication interface routines. This library contains user callable routines for message passing and spawning remote processes. The communication subsystem currently only supports the TCP/IP [Tanenbaum, 1981] [Comer and Stevens, 1993] protocol, and therefore broadcasting is only simulated; it does not take advantage of the broadcast medium of network such as Ethernet. An extension of the communication subsystem to support a reliable broadcast protocol [Kaashoek et al., 1989] [Kaashoek et al., 1993] using UDP/IP is currently under development.

The daemon is a local binding service and enables clients (e.g., protected objects) to locate the address of servers (e.g., sequencers). When a server starts up, it registers its address with the local daemon. When a client starts up, it finds out the server's address by making a request to all the daemons of the virtual machine.

The communication library provides the following services:

- *Startup*: Enrolls a process in the local daemon.

- *Cleanup*: Deregisters a process from the local daemon.

- *Open*: Opens a communication channel (Send or Receive mode).

- *Close*: Closes a communication channel.

- *Recv*: Receives a message from a given communication channel.

- *Send*: Sends a message to a given communication channel.

- *Trans*: Sends and receives a message atomically.

- *CreateRemoteProcess*: Creates a virtual node on a remote host.

4.6 Example - The Traveling Salesperson Problem

The classic problem of the traveling salesperson (TSP) is to find the shortest route for a salesperson to visit (exactly once) each of the *n* cities of his territory. The problem can be solved using a *branch-and-bound* algorithm. And a sequential solution is given by [Horowitz and Sahni, 1978]. Briefly, the algorithm organizes the solution space into a *tree*. Each leaf node *L* is a solution and represents the tours defined by the path from the root to *L*. A *branching function* defines how the tree is built, while a *bounding function* is used to avoid the generation of subtrees that do not contain a solution (i.e., a shortest route). For the TSP, the bounding function is simple. If the length of a partial tour exceeds the length of any already calculated tour, the partial tour will never lead to a solution better than what is already known. It is easy to see that subtrees can be expanded in parallel.

[Bal and al., 1990a] gives a distributed solution which searches the branches of the tree in parallel. The solution is based on the replicated worker paradigm where a *manager* task places work into a queue for some *workers* to process. The manager task generates partial tours for the salesperson up to a given depth. The worker tasks further expand these partial tours systematically until all possible tours are generated. Given a partial tour, the worker checks whether it is better than the current shortest tour. Every time a worker finds a shorter tour, it updates a protected object shared among all worker tasks, and the protected object contains the length of the shortest tour so far. This protected object is used to cut-off partial tours that are already longer than the current shortest tour, as these will never lead to an optimal solution.

As a proof-of-concept, we have performed preliminary performance measurements on a distributed system containing three 486 based machines running under the Windows NT ™ operating system connected by a 10 Mbit/sec Ethernet. The test was limited to only three machines since broadcasting is currently only simulated. The performances are determined by measuring the program execution time for solving two randomly generated input graphs with 16 cities each. The manager process searches three levels of the tree, so it generates $15 \times 14 \times 13 = 2730$ partial tours which are then expanded by the workers. Table 1 shows the speedups obtained for these problems. The distributed implementation of this program is far from being as efficient as the Orca implementation presented by [Bal, 1990a]. There are two main reasons for this difference. First, the Orca communication protocol [Kaashoek et al., 1989] is implemented in the operating system kernel space or directly on top of the hardware; the Ada communication protocol is implemented in the user space. Second, the Ada communication protocol is currently only simulated and uses

TCP/IP, a byte-stream protocol not adapted for a system performing mostly small RPCs.

Table 4.1: TSP Performance Measurements

	First problem		Second problem	
#Hosts	Time (sec)	Speedup	Time (sec)	Speedup
1	879	1.00	1475	1.00
2	508	1.73	829	1.78
3	371	2.37	583	2.53

Chapter 5

Conclusion

Distributed applications become more and more difficult to program. As a consequence, programming languages with higher levels of abstraction must be provided to the programmer. The first part of the thesis described some popular distributed programming languages and showed the advantages of data sharing over message passing.

The second part of the thesis presented how Ada can be used to program distributed systems, then showed how important it is to support synchronization conditions and to retain the syntax of the protected objects in a distributed environment. Since Ada 95 restricts protected objects to being entry-less, a new model based on data sharing and making use of protected objects was introduced. Replication is a key to providing good performance. The implementation of the model automatically replicates protected objects to allow each task to directly read a local copy on its virtual node. For a write operation, all replicated protected objects are updated by broadcasting the operation. Also, state information such as barrier conditions and the number of tasks waiting on an entry queue (the Count attribute) are kept consistent on each virtual node. The model concluded that most of the syntax of the protected objects can be maintained in a distributed environment. Several restrictions (not surprisingly) were also found to be necessary to implement the model.

The communication subsystem allowing distributed entities to communicate with each other and a detailed example with some performance results were also presented. The example showed that the model is easy to program and presents excellent performances for applications where the ratio of the number of read operations to the number of write operations is high.

The model made use of an Ada 83 compiler, and some issues such as passing protected objects as arguments in remote protected operation call and ATC were not addressed. We have not investigated to see if these issues could be resolved using an Ada 95 compiler. Several improvements should be possible using an Ada 95 compiler. Future work could consist of introducing a *read only* pragma for read only entries which Count attribute is not referenced and determining whether it is possible to transform protected objects into protected objects that retain their limited type characteristics. A fault tolerant implementation of the pre-translator where replicated objects could be used to increase fault-tolerance as well as to decrease the access cost to the objects is another possibility.

Finally, it should also be feasible to implement a similar model where partitions instead of tasks communicate with each other through protected objects. Such a model would be viewed as complement to the Ada 95 Distributed Annex since, the shared memory paradigm only supports entry-less protected objects.

Appendix

The Traveling Salesperson Problem

The following is a complete listing of the original code for the Traveling Salesperson

Problem.

The Traveling Salesperson Problem Original Code

```
package TSPTypes is

  MaxHops : constant INTEGER := 3;
  NrTowns : constant INTEGER := 16;

  type PAIR is record
    ToCity : INTEGER;
    dist   : INTEGER;
  end record;

  type DISTARRAY is array ( 1 .. NrTowns ) of PAIR;
  type DISTTAB   is array ( 1 .. NrTowns ) of DISTARRAY;

  type PATHTYPE is array ( 1 .. NrTowns ) of INTEGER;
  type JOBTYPE is record
    len  : INTEGER;
    path : PATHTYPE;
  end record;

end TSPTypes;
```

```
with TSPTypes;
use  TSPTypes;
with Queue;
package JobQueue is

  pragma distributed( Node => Node_0);
  protected JobQueue is

    procedure AddJob( job : JOBTYPE);
    procedure NoMoreJobs;
    entry GetJob( job : out JOBTYPE; F : out BOOLEAN);

  private

    package JobQueue is new Queue(JOBTYPE);
    done : BOOLEAN := FALSE;
    Q     : QUEUE;

  end JobQueue;

end JobQueue;

package body JobQueue is

  protected body JobQueue is

    procedure AddJob( job : JOBTYPE) is
    begin
      JobQueue.Add( The_Item => job, To_The_Queue => Q );
    end AddJob;

    procedure NoMoreJobs is
    begin
      done := TRUE;
    end NoMoreJobs;

    entry GetJob( job : out JOBTYPE; F : out BOOLEAN)
      when ( not JobQueue.Is_Empty(Q) or ( done and JobQueue.Is_Empty(Q) ) ) is
      p : ItemName;
    begin
      if not JobQueue.Is_Empty(Q) then
        job := JobQueue.Front_Of(Q);
        JobQueue.Pop(Q);
        F := TRUE;
      else -- ( done and Q.First = NULL)
        F := FALSE;
      end if;
    end GetJob;

  end JobQueue;

end JobQueue;
```

```
package IntObject is

  pragma distributed( Node => Node_0);
  protected type IntObject( Value : INTEGER := 0) is
    function Value return INTEGER;
    procedure Assign( V : in INTEGER);
    procedure Min( V : in INTEGER);
    procedure Inc;
    procedure Dec;
    entry AwaitZero;
  private
    X : INTEGER := Value;
  end IntObject;

end IntObject;

package body IntObject is

  protected type body IntObject is
    function Value return INTEGER is
    begin
      return X;
    end Value;

    procedure Assign( V : in INTEGER) is
    begin
      X := V;
    end Assign;

    procedure Min( V : in INTEGER) is
    begin
      if V < X then
        X := V;
      end if;
    end Min;

    procedure Inc is
    begin
      X := X + 1;
    end Inc;

    procedure Dec is
    begin
      X := X - 1;
    end Dec;

    entry AwaitZero when X = 0 is
    begin
      null;
    end AwaitZero;

  end IntObject;

end IntObject;
```

```
with Text_IO;
with Ada_Numerics_Random_Numbers;
use  Ada_Numerics_Random_Numbers;
with TspTypes;
use  TspTypes;
with JobQueue;
use  JobQueue;
with IntObject;
use  IntObject;
procedure tsp is

  package minimum      is new IntObject.IntObject(INTEGER'LAST);
  package WorkersActive is new IntObject.IntObject(2); -- 2 is the number of workers

  pragma distributed
    ( Node                 => Node_0,
      With_Packages        => (...), -- must create a package containing present and tsp
      With_Protected_Objects => (minimum, WorkersActive) );
  task type Worker is
    entry Go( dist : in DISTTAB);
  end Worker;

  pragma redistributed( Node => Node_0);
  Worker0 : Worker;
  pragma redistributed( Node => Node_1);
  Worker1 : Worker;
  -- other workers should be declared here

  distance : DISTTAB;

  function present(city, hops : INTEGER; path : PATHTYPE) return BOOLEAN is
  begin
    for I in 1 .. hops loop
      if path(i) = city then
        return TRUE;
      end if;
    end loop;
    return FALSE;
  end present;

  procedure tsp
    ( hops     : INTEGER;
      len      : INTEGER;
      path     : in out PATHTYPE;
      distance : DISTTAB ) is
    city, dist, me : INTEGER;
  begin
    if len >= minimum.value then
      null;
    elsif hops = NrTowns then
      -- min is always decremented, this artifact
      -- reduces the number of write operations
      -- since Ada only allows a single guard expression per entry
      if len < minimum.value then
```

```
      minimum.min(len);
    end if;
  else
    me := path(hops);
    for I in 1 .. NrTowns loop
      city := distance(me)(I).ToCity;
      if not present(city, hops, path) then
        path(hops+1) := city;
        dist := distance(me)(I).dist;
        tsp(hops+1, len+dist, path, distance);
      end if;
    end loop;
  end if;
end tsp;


procedure distributor
  ( hops    : INTEGER;
    len     : INTEGER;
    path    : in out PATHTYPE;
    distance : DISTTAB ) is
  city, dist, me : INTEGER;
begin
  if hops = MaxHops then
    JobQueue.JobQueue.AddJob( (len, path) );
  else
    me := path(hops);
    for I in 1 .. NrTowns loop
      city := distance(me)(I).ToCity;
      if not present(city,hops,path) then
        path(hops+1) := city;
        dist := distance(me)(I).dist;
        distributor(hops+1, len+dist, path, distance);
      end if;
    end loop;
  end if;
end distributor;


procedure GenerateJobs(distance : DistTab) is
  path : PATHTYPE;
begin
  path(1) := 1;
  distributor(1, 0, path, distance);
  JobQueue.JobQueue.NoMoreJobs;
end GenerateJobs;


procedure InitDistance( distance : out DISTTAB) is
  Gen : Generator;
begin
  for I in 1 .. NrTowns loop
    for J in 1 .. NrTowns loop
      distance(I)(J).ToCity := J;
      distance(I)(J).dist := Random_Integer( Gen, 1, 100);
    end loop;
  end loop;
```

```
    end InitDistance;

    task body Worker is
      job      : JobType;
      F        : BOOLEAN;
      distance : DISTTAB;
    begin
      accept Go( dist : in DISTTAB) do
        distance := dist;
      end Go;
      loop
        JobQueue.JobQueue.GetJob(job,F);
        exit when not F;
        tsp( MaxHops, job.len, job.path, distance );
      end loop;
      WorkersActive.dec;
    end Worker;

begin -- tsp
  InitDistance(distance);
  Worker1.Go(distance);
  GenerateJobs(distance);
  Worker0.Go(distance);
  WorkersActive.AwaitZero;
  Text_IO.Put_Line( INTEGER'IMAGE( minimum.value ) );
end tsp;
```

References

Ada 95 Reference Manual, Version 6.0, Mapping/Revision Team, Intermetrics, ANSI/ISO DIS 8652:1995, *December 1994.*

Ada 95 Rationale, Version 6.0, Mapping/Revision Team, Intermetrics,*December 1994.*

Annotated Ada 95 Reference Manual, Version 6.0, Mapping/Revision Team, Intermetrics, *December 1994.*

Ahuja, S., Carriero, N. and Gelernter, D. "Linda and Friends." *IEEE Computer, pp. 26-34, August 1986.*

Andrew, G.R., et al. "An Overview of the SR Language and Implementation." *ACM Transactions on Programming Languages and Systems, Vol. 10, No. 1, pp. 51-86, January 1988.*

ANSI 1983, Reference Manual for the Ada Programming Language. ANSI/MIL Std-1815A, 1983.

Atkinson, C., Moreton, T., and Natali, A. Ada for Distributed Systems. *Cambridge University Press, 1988.*

Atkinson, C., and Goldsack, S.J. "Communication between Ada Programs in DIADEM." *ACM Ada Letters, Vol. 8, No. 7, pp. 86-96, 1988 Special Edition .*

Atkinson, C., Di Maio, A., and Bayan, R. "DRAGOON: An Object-Oriented Notation supporting the Reuse and Distribution of Ada Software." *ACM Ada Letters, Vol. 10, No. 9, pp. 50-59, Fall 1990.*

Atkinson, C. Object-Oriented Reuse, Concurrency and Distribution, an Ada-based Approach. Reading, MA, Addison-Wesley, 1991.

Bal, H.E., and Tanenbaum, A.S. "Distributed Programming with Shared Data." *Proc. IEEE CS 1988 Int. Conf on Computer Languages, pp.82-91, October 1988.*

Bal, H.E., Steiner, J.G., and Tanenbaum, A.S. "Programming Languages for Distributed Computing Systems." *ACM Computing Surveys, Vol. 21, No. 3, pp. 261-322, September 1989.*

Bal, H.E. Programming Distributed Systems. *Summit, N.J. Silicon Press, 1990.*

Bal, H.E., Kaashoek, M.F., and Tanenbaum, A.S. "Experience with Distributed Programming in Orca." *Proc. IEEE CS 1990 int. Conf on Computer Languages, pp.79-89, March 1990.*

Bal, H.E., Kaashoek, M.F., and Tanenbaum, A.S. "Orca: A Language for Distributed Programming." *ACM SIGPLAN Notices, Vol. 25, No. 5, May 1990.*

Bal, H.E., Kaashoek, M.F., and Tanenbaum, A.S. "Orca: A Language for Parallel Programming of Distributed Systems." *IEEE Transactions on Software Engineering, Vol. 18, No. 3, pp. 190-205, March 1992.*

Bal, H.E., Kaashoek, M.F., and Tanenbaum, A.S. "Replication techniques for Speeding up Parallel Applications on Distributed Systems." *Concurrency-Practice and Experience, Vol. 4, No. 5, pp. 337-355, August 1992.*

Bal, H.E., and Kaashoek, M.F. "Object Distribution in Orca using Compile-Time and Run-Time Techniques." *Proc. Eighth Annual Conference On Object-Oriented Programming Systems, Languages, and Application, OOPSLA'93.*

Bal, H.E., and Athanasiu, I. "The Arc Consistency Problem: a Case Study in Parallel Programming with Shared Objects." *Seventh International Conference on Parallel and Distributed Computing Systems, October 1994.*

Bal, H.E., "Comparing Data Synchronization in Ada 9X and Orca." *ACM Ada Letters, Vol. 14, No. 1, pp. 50-63, January 1995.*

Barnes, J.G.P. Programming in Ada, Plus an Overview of Ada 9X, 4th ed., *Reading MA, Addison-Wesley, 1994.*

Birrell, A.D., and Nelson, B.J. "Implementing Remote Procedure Calls." *ACM Transactions on Computer Systems, Vol. 2, No.1, pp. 39-59, February 1984.*

Birman, K.P., and Van Renesse, R. Reliable Distributed Computing with the Isis Toolkit. *IEEE Computer Society Press, 1994.*

Bishop, J.M, et al. "Distributing Concurrent Ada Programs by Source Translation." *Software-Practice and Experience, Vol. 17(12), pp.859-884, December 1987.*

Bishop, J.M, "Three Steps to Distribution: Partitioning, Configuring and Adapting." *Ada Letters, 1988 Special Edition, pp. 97-100, 1988.*

Black, A., et al. "Distribution and Abstract Types in Emerald." *IEEE Transaction on Software Engineering, Vol. SE-13, No. 1, pp. 65-76, January 1987.*

Brinch Hansen, P. "Distributed Processes: A Concurrent Programming Concept." *Communications of the ACM, Vol. 21, No. 11, pp. 934-941, November 1978.*

Burns, A. and Davies, G.L. "Ada 9X Protected Types in Pascal-FC." *ACM Ada Letters, Vol. 12, No. 6, pp. 59-74, November 1992.*

Carriero, N., and Gerlernter, D. "Linda in Context." *Communication of the ACM, Vol. 32, No. 4, pp. 444-458, April 1989.*

Comer, D.E., and Stevens, D.L. Internetworking with TCP/IP. *Prentice-Hall, Englewood Cliffs, N.J., 1993.*

Dasgupta, et al. "The Clouds Distributed Operating Systems." *IEEE Computer, Vol. 24, No. 11, pp. 34-44, November 1991.*

Dobbing, B. "Distributed Ada, A Suggested Solution For Ada 9X." *ACM Ada Letters, Vol. 10, No. 9, pp. 94-102, Fall 1990.*

Dobbing, B. "Experiences with the Partitions Model." *ACM Ada Letters, Vol. 13, No. 2, pp. 65-77, March 1993.*

Eisenhauer, G., et al. "An Implementation Supporting Distributed Execution of Partitioned Ada Programs." *ACM Ada Letters, Vol. 9, No. 1, pp. 147-160, January 1989.*

Eisenhauer, G., et al. "Targeting a Traditional Compiler to a Distributed Environment." *ACM Ada Letters, Vol. 9, No. 2., pp. 45-51, March 1989.*

Fisher, D.A., and Weatherly, R.M. "Issues in the Design of a Distributed Operating System for Ada." *IEEE Computer, Vol. 19, No. 5, pp. 38-47, May 1986.*

Gargaro, A.B., et al. "Supporting Distribution and Dynamic Reconfiguration in AdaPT." *Distributed Systems Engineering, Vol. 1, pp. 145-161, 1994.*

Gargaro, A.B., Kermarrec, Y., Pautet, L., and Tardieu, S. "Paris - Partitioned Ada for Remotely Invoked Services." *Technical Report 95008-info, ENST-Bretagne, March 1995.*

Gehani, N.H. "Concurrency in Ada and Multicomputers." *Computer Languages, Vol. 7. pp. 21-23, 1982.*

78

Gehani, N.H. "Capsules: A Shared Memory Access Mechanism for Concurrent C/C++." *IEEE Transactions on Parallel and Distributed Systems, Vol. 4, No. 7, pp. 795-811, July 1993.*

Giering, E.W., and Baker, T.P. "Ada 9X Asynchronous Transfer Of Control: Applications And Implementation." *ACM SIGPLAN Workshop on Language, Compiler, and Tool Support for Real-Time Systems, June 1994.*

Goldsack, S.J., et al. "Translating an AdaPT Partition to Ada9X." *ACM Ada Letters, Vol. 13, No. 2, pp. 78-90, March 1993.*

Goldsack, S.J., et al. "AdaPT and Ada9X." *ACM Ada Letters, Vol. 14, No. 2, pp. 80-92, March 1994.*

Gunaseelan, L., and LeBlanc, R.J., "Distributed Eiffel: A Language for Programming Multi-Granular Distributed Objects on the Clouds Operating System." *Proc. IEEE CS 1992, Int. Conf. on Computer Languages.*

Hartley, C.L., and Sunderam, V.S. "Concurrent Programming with Shared Objects in Network Environments." *International Parallel Proceedings Symposium, April 1993.*

Helary, J.M., et al. "Detection of Stable Properties in Distributed Applications." *Proc. 6th ACM Symp. on Principles of Distributed Computing, pp. 125-136, 1987.*

Hoare, C.A.R. "Communicating Sequential Processes." *Communications of the ACM, Vol. 21, No. 11, pp. 666-677, August 1978.*

Horowitz, E. and Sahni, S. Fundamentals of Computer Algorithms. Potomac, Maryland. Computer Science Press, 1978.

Hudak, P. "Para-Functional Programming." *IEEE Computer, Vol. 19, No. 8, pp. 60-70, August 1986.*

Hutcheon, A., and Wellings, A.J. "The York Distributed Ada Project." *Proceedings of the Distributed Ada'89 Symposium, pp. 67-104.*

Inmos ltd. Occam Programming Manual.*Prentice-Hall, Englewood Cliffs, N.J., 1984.*

Jessop, W.H. "Ada Packages and Distributed Systems." *SIGPLAN Notices, February 1982.*

Jha, R. et al. "Ada Program Partitioning Language: A Notation for Distributing Ada Programs." *IEEE Transactions on Software Engineering, Vol. 15, No. 3, pp. 271-280, March 1989.*

Kaashoek, M.F., et al. "An Efficient Reliable Broadcast Protocol." *Operating Systems Review, Vol. 23, pp. 5-19, Oct 1989.*

Kaashoek, M.F., et al. "FLIP: An Internetwork Protocol for Supporting Distributed Systems." *ACM Transactions on Computer Systems, Vol. 11, No. 1, pp. 73-106, February 1993.*

Kermarrec, Y., and Pautet, L. "Evaluation of the Distributed Annex of Ada 9X and its Implementation in GNAT." *Technical Report 94009-info, ENST-Bretagne, February 1994.*

Ledru, P. "Translation of the Protected Type Mechanism in Ada 83." *ACM Ada Letters, Vol. 15, No. 1, pp. 64-69, January 1995.*

Ledru, P. "Protected Types with Entry Barriers Depending on Parameters of the Entries: Some Practical Examples." *ACM Ada Letters, Vol. 15, No. 4, pp. 46-49, July 1995.*

Levelt, W.G., Bal, H.E., Kaashoek, M.F., and Tanenbaum, A.S. "A Comparison of Two Paradigms for Distributed Shared Memory." *Software-Practice and Experience, Vol. 22, No. 11, pp. 985-1010, November 1992.*

Nitzberg, B., and Lo, V. "Distributed Shared Memory: A Survey of Issues and Algorithms." *IEEE Computer, pp. 52-60, August 1991.*

Sunderam, V.S. "PVM: A Framework for Parallel Distributed Computing." *Concurrency-Practice and Experience, Vol. 2, No. 4, December 1990.*

Tanenbaum, A.S. Computer Networks. *Prentice-Hall, 1981.*

Tanenbaum, A.S., Kaashoek, M.F., and Bal, H.E. "Parallel Programming Using Shared Objects and Broadcasting." *IEEE Computer, pp. 10-19, August 1992.*

Tedd, M., Crespi-Reghizzi, S., and Natali, A. Ada for Multi-Microprocessors. *Cambridge University Press, 1984.*

Volz, R.A., et al. "Some Problems in Distributed Real-Time Ada Programs Across Machines." *Proceedings of the Ada International Conference, 1985 pp. 72-84, 1985.*

Volz, R.A., and Mudge, T.N. "Timing Issues in the Distributed Execution of Ada Programs." *IEEE Transactions on Computers, Vol. C-36, No.4, pp. 449-459, April 1987.*

Volz, R.A., et al. "Translation and Execution of Distributed Ada Programs: Is it Still Ada?" *IEEE Transactions on Software Engineering, Vol. 15, No. 3, pp. 281-292, March 1989.*

Volz, R.A. "Virtual Nodes and Units of Distribution for Distributed Ada." *ACM Ada Letters, Vol. 10, No. 4, pp. 85-96, Spring 1990.*

Volz, R.A. et al. "Distributed and Parallel Ada and the Ada 9X Recommendations." *Distributed Systems Engineering, Vol. 1, pp. 224-241, 1994.*

Volz, R.A., et al. "Distributed and Parallel Execution in Ada 83." *Proceedings of the Third Workshop on Parallel and Distributed Real-Time Systems, pp. 52-61, April 1995.*

Wellings, A.J. "Distributed Execution, Units of Partitioning." *ACM Ada Letters, Vol. 8, No. 7, pp. 80-85, 1988 Special Edition.*

Notes